An Extraordinary Ordinary Life

Insights from Parenting a Disabled Child

LUCY MUELLER

An Extraordinary/Ordinary Life
Insights from Parenting a Disabled Child

Book design by StoriesToTellBooks.com

An Extraordinary Ordinary Life

Insights from Parenting a Disabled Child

Contents

"Balance: Seeing the Extraordinary in the Ordinary

This book contains reflections of how I have struggled—and continue to struggle—to balance being a woman, a partner, a daughter, a teacher, an art therapist, a citizen, and a mother of two amazing individuals, one, a son with disabilities. Thank you to all parents, families, friends, educators, medical personnel, and human service workers—the caring network.

This book contains selections from my diaries, journals, and daybooks, as well as memoirs created in writing groups. The paragraphs that appear in *italics* are my exact words as written at the time. Each entry references a date to place it in some chronology and give the reader some idea of the amount of time that has elapsed since the actual events occurred. Very few writings were written specifically with this book in mind. All writings are my own.

The illustrations are my paintings and drawings that graphically represent emotions I may not have been able to put into words. The images here are about releasing and expressing my emotional and physical pain or joy; they were created quickly as art as therapy and never meant to be finished artworks. Photographs are from my photo albums and more recent digital pictures. Family photos are included with permission and to show Curt's life as normal. All words and images are my own.

The organization of this book is not chronological. Knowing that it may be read by anyone, from parents who are intimately involved to teachers or medical personnel, I decided to organize the book in expanding circles: it starts with the parent/caregiver, moves to the child, expands to extended family, includes some of the many organizations that are involved in the child's care, and ends with various practical suggestions.

Because the English language has no gender-neutral pronouns to describe a single person, I use male pronouns throughout because my child is a male. Names are substitutes for the real people represented, except my son, Curt, and his sister, Laura.

Medical terms and references cited can be found in the Glossary and References/Inspiration sections. Many terms have been used to describe people with disabilities. I have used "People First" language, which addresses the person first then the disability; i.e., "a person with an intellectual disability," or "a person who uses a wheelchair."

I have tried to be respectful throughout this writing. All errors of perception, descriptions of events, and judgments are my own, as are the insights herein. I am a slow but steady learner, but I have had an exceptional teacher. Thank you to Curt and the rest of my family and to the many individuals who have cared for us.

Mother and Son

Brother and Sister

Instructions for Living a Life

Pay attention. Be astonished. Tell about it.
~Mary Oliver

Days of Ordinary Life and the Day My Life Changed

In this book I would like to both relate my story and tell what I have learned from it, with the hope there will be something in it that will help you if you are the parent of a child with disabilities. Each child born with disabilities is different. My son's disabilities are very serious, but not as much as those of other individuals I have met. On the other side, many of you may have a child with much milder disabilities. In any case, whatever the degree of the problems, I believe these insights about raising a child with disabilities are applicable.

I'm a born list maker and diary keeper. Not long ago I found my 1970 diary, as well as others from the subsequent years, in a tattered box marked "Curt." I hesitated to open that diary, knowing how dramatically my life changed in June of 1970. That year my son, Curt, was born with a rare chromosome abnormality that caused various and serious disabilities. His diagnoses included failure to thrive, epilepsy, psychomotor retardation, and extreme valgus foot deformities; he has no self-preservation skills and is almost non-verbal. He has always needed 24-hour supervision. Acknowledging the seriousness of his limitations and the effects upon my life, the contents of those accumulated writings really surprised me; they included many things, but the things unsaid were probably most significant.

The first entry of that year was a list of people to notify of our change of address. My husband and I had recently left military life and moved to be closer to family when I discovered I was pregnant. Most of the notes were about the move:

> *slacks to cleaners*
> *paint molding*
> *line shelves*
> *2nd coat*
> *get doc recommendations*
> *telephone company*

Plus, there were almost daily menus:

> *steak fried*
> *baked potatoes*
> *limas*
> *fruit jello*
> *spare ribs*
> *rice*
> *spinach*
> *jello salad*
> *tuna casserole*
> *coleslaw*
> *corn*
> *veg soup*

There were notes of visits to my parents, my husband's travel schedule, days that had no notations, details of presents I was making for loved ones, OB visits, housecleaning chores, a few social dates with people I can't even remember, notes about sewing projects, and more menus. In June the entries got fewer: *meat pies, chicken livers and onions.* My sister's anniversary was listed, my brother's graduation, doctor's visit on June 9th. I remember I was about 155 pounds and 55" around the belly; I looked like I'd swallowed a watermelon, but no mention of any of this. Blank pages, then June 11th, my sister's birthday.

Saturday June 13's entry was:

> *Curt born 10:15 PM.*

Then blank pages until:

> *June 17: brought Curt home.*
> *June 21: Father's Day: eggplant.*
> *June 24: Curt to hospital.*
> *June 27: we fed him.*
> *June 30: brought him home.*

Then more blank pages until:

> *July 9: anniversary, steak, champagne.*
> *July 10: pack Curt's things, pack for Lucy, wash, cash*
> for our first trip away from home with our son.

Slowly, the pages began to fill again but with some new additions to the entries:

> *July 20: Dr. F. chromosome tests.*
> *July 28: Drs. G, F, etc.*

Sometimes, there was a medical appointment every week. Curiously, there were some interesting entries:

> *Aug 12: deliver Curt to Mom.*
> *Aug 13: Washington.*
> *Aug 15: reunion.*
> *Aug 17: pick up Curt.*

That was five days! He was two months old. Curt was a happy baby; my mom loved him, read to him, made funny noises with him, and his father and I got away together.

The rest of that year was much the same as before Curt was born, except fewer entries in general:

Dec 8: call for apt for Curt, liquor store, mail package, Curt has seizure.

Thereafter, neurologists were added to the list of appointments, along with EEGs and medication notes.

Astonishingly, there was no mention of the fact that Curt almost died when he was 10 days old. He had lost three pounds and was severely dehydrated by the time we took him to the emergency room that day. The doctor tried four places to get an IV into him and finally got one in his shriveled umbilical cord. Curt recovered, and we brought him home six days later, as noted.

A week thereafter, we had a post-hospital visit to the pediatricians, who then told us that our son "would be a vegetable" and it would "be better to put him away and forget about him." That was an extraordinarily horrible event! Perhaps that information was just too painful to write in a diary, but it is a glaring omission that I noticed in reviewing my diary entries in preparation for writing this book. I have often wondered if the pediatricians suspected that something was wrong when Curt was born but just didn't mention it, hoping their suspicions were unwarranted. In retrospect, their quick diagnosis after he failed to thrive certainly has raised my suspicions, but at the time I was just shocked and upset and obviously did not write about it in my diary.

I'd been dreading reading these old notebooks but have found great relief to discover the beginnings of the patterns that have continued throughout our family life. For example, I have always called my son Curt or Curtis, plus some descriptive nicknames, but never "Baby," much less "Poor Baby." In spite of the struggles, I have never seen his life as a tragedy, any more than I ever considered it a special blessing or particularly amazing in any way. My family has been tremendously important; I love cooking and making presents for others, and I believe life is worth recording, that leaving a written record of events is important. Ironically, life is the ordinary details: tuna casseroles and doctors' appointments are perhaps equally revealing in the long run.

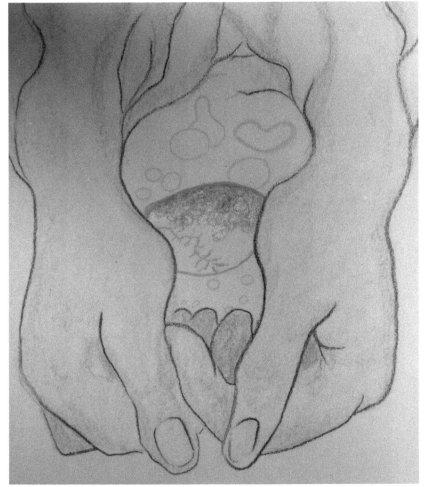

"Fragile"

"I don't know how you do it"

How many times have I heard that phrase in the years since Curt was born? In the early years, if a stranger looked away, quickly scurried off, or turned her cart abruptly into the next aisle of the supermarket when she saw me trying to guide the cart that my son, Curtis, was gleefully but erratically pushing around, I would take a deep breath and try to smile. But there were some who would look up, briefly catch my eye and mouth, "God bless you!" before they moved on. But when there was just a little more time and the conversation got going, I often heard, "I couldn't do it!" But we do. Most of the hundreds of thousands—perhaps millions of us—who have raised a child with special needs, developmental delays, intellectual impairment, or whatever anything different is called, we actually just do it, but we do it in various ways.

This book is not a "How To" or "You've Been Blessed" book. If you are responsible for someone with special needs for his lifetime, you won't have much time to read, but perhaps these words will help. Now that I'm in my 70s, I finally have the time and the interest in writing down my memories and theories of 50 years of parenting. We all react differently, depending upon our background, the medical and social environment in which we live, our social-economic status, our family support or lack thereof, the state we live in, our own physical and mental health, and the personality of the person who is our 24-hour responsibility. We mess up, we make mistakes, we scream, rage, pray, weep, withdraw, over eat, under eat, blame, beg, and wonder how we'll get through each day, but we do. Time moves on, things change, we change, our child lives or dies.

These are some notes, a few revelations, and some practical tips about what I've learned and how I manage. It isn't easy, but it's not as impossible as it may seem to others. There are tremendous rewards, huge sacrifices, daily challenges, and opportunities each minute. Yours is probably not an "angel child," and this is not about what I call being a Martyr Mother.

Do you know the movie "Awakening" (1990) with Robert De Niro and Robin Williams? In the movie, the doctor (Williams) develops some magic formula that arouses the patient (De Niro) from a coma he's been in for 30 years. The mother in the film fits my idea of a Martyr Mother; she has meaning and a role in life when she has to take care of her son. After years of being cared for like a baby by this adoring mother, De Niro awakens to consciousness, full activity, and a complete, adult, emotional and psychological life. What a change for him and the mother! When he "awakens" and goes off on his own, she is lost and confused. At the end of the movie, the magic formula wears off, and De Niro and others who benefited from the miracle regress and return to their vegetative states. The mother resumes her role with energy and purposefulness.

I chose not to devote my whole life to my son, but I have often thought of that movie and wondered what my son would say if he were ever able to talk. So I try to always treat him like a person who comprehends everything I say and who has a right to express opinions about things that matter in his life.

This book is about the whole of it. Yes, you have a child with special needs/disabilities/challenges, but you do not need to believe any of the stereotypes that are in your head (or in your mother-in-law's head!) You have other people in your life and a life of your own that is important. It's a balance every minute, but the goal is love. Each of us has special needs, and that includes you and the other members of your family.

CHAPTER 1

You

Everybody's fighting some kind of stereotype, and people with disabilities are no exception. The difference is that barriers people with disabilities face begin with people's attitudes—attitudes often rooted in misinformation and misunderstandings about what it's like to live with a disability.

~Easterseals.com

This chapter is about caring for your child with disabilities, your family, and yourself by caring for yourself—if not first, at least as much as you possibly can. How does the stress affect your body, mind, and spirit? You can choose your role, even change your role as your child grows, but it's all about balance.

Your attitude toward the events of your life is your choice, even if you have no control over some of the events that unfold. You will learn to determine what actions you can control and develop a belief/practice about how to cope with what you can't control. This is the first chapter for a good reason.

Resisting the Martyr Mother Syndrome

How easily I recognize it now but how difficult it was to pull myself away from the role of Martyr Mother. It's a dramatic and all-consuming role, one that pulls out all the mothering instincts and survival skills I didn't even know I had. It's a 24-hour job, and your mind, body, and spirit are totally dedicated to taking the best care possible of your child. People admire you. Everyone certainly has some relative or friend who has some type of disability, so the connections are easy to make, comparisons sometimes helpful, and the compassion wholehearted and comforting. It's particularly rewarding to be a Martyr Mother if your family or partner is not very supportive or if you are a single parent. Having a child with disabilities puts additional stress on a marriage or partnership. It adds worries, often makes physical demands of care, and challenges priorities that used to involve just the two of you. It's difficult to manage the extra responsibilities, the fears, and the worries while trying to maintain or strengthen the marriage. Becoming the sole caregiver, either because your partner won't help or because you two can't work out a way to share the chores and worries, quickly draws you to others with similar life issues and makes it easier to be a Martyr Mother and attempt to take on all responsibilities yourself. It becomes your job, your life, your purpose for living, for dragging yourself out of bed very morning and, probably, five times during the night. It seems there is no other choice. If you are going to make the best life possible for your special child, you need to give it your all, right? Not necessarily.

When Curtis was about seven years old, I was working as the resource room director in an amazing, experimental preschool for severely disabled children and "temporarily able-bodied" peers. Both Curt and his younger sister, Laura, attended it and loved the challenging and stimulating program. Suffice it to say, I was officially working in a job that meant total focus on children with disabilities. It was exhilarating; it was exhausting; it was all-consuming.

One day when I was very, very tired, I was talking to my boss, a wise and compassionate woman named Kathleen. I said that

I was exhausted and was considering quitting. Kathleen asked, "And what do you want to do next?"

Without hesitating and with no conscious thought of even considering my answer and my future, I replied, "I want to do something with my art."

Kathleen's immediate response was, "Wonderful! I was hoping you would say that!"

That was a turning point. After that afternoon I began to notice that all of my attention was on disability issues. My thoughts and my conversation centered on individuals who were struggling with cerebral palsy, Down syndrome or with lack of a limb—it was the time when mothers who had been given the sedative thalidomide gave birth to children with terrible birth deformities. One night we were at a party, and I watched myself and listened to my own conversation. Yes, indeed, my interactions were intense and meaningful and often took place huddled in a corner, but other people at the party were in larger groups, laughing, talking, and seeming to ignore those of us who were "more serious." I wasn't fun to be with. That was an uncomfortable self-awareness that took a long time to change and still remains a challenge for me.

I didn't have to be a full-time mother and assume the full responsibility or become a professional mother of a disabled child. The balancing took years. Curt's father and I were unable to develop a system of communication and a sharing of responsibilities, and our marriage failed, but both Curt and I matured, and our roles changed, not only because of a better understanding of myself—and regular therapy—but also because my son matured and became a man and naturally moved away from home. The process was normal and predictable but required time, work, and trust. (See Chapter 3. US: FAMILY.) Now, my son has lived *away* from home longer than he lived *at* home with my 24-hour-a-day supervision.

There are now days when I don't even think of my son—or my daughter—when my full attention is on the garden, my art projects, or the music for an upcoming chorale concert. It was a hard lesson to learn. My life, my son's, and, hopefully, my daughter's lives have been richer because I didn't make *his* life *my* life.

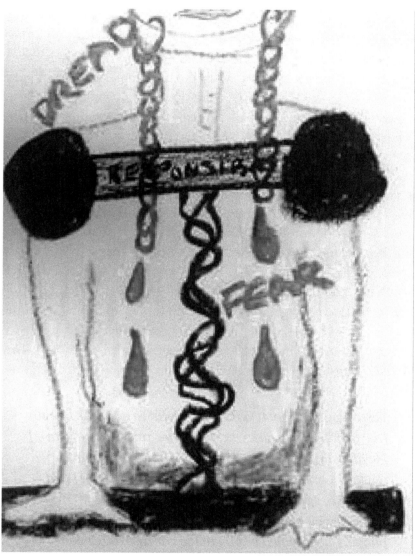

"Dread, Responsibility, Fear"

Guilt, Worry, and the Struggle for Emotional Balance

I was not brought up in an expressive family. My parents were of Germanic descent and from the Midwest. We did not shout, cry, scream, moan, hiccup, hum, or burp loudly, much less flap our hands in glee. Education, intelligence, and intellectual curiosity were valued, and quiet activities were encouraged. We knew we were loved, but emotions were always kept in check. We didn't experience guilt, but we knew what was expected of us. We were happy growing up, but I didn't know how to deal with my very mixed feelings about the fragile, funny, little boy who became my responsibility. Any emotional balance I've achieved came from learning how to recognize and appropriately balance my emotions. Guilt and worry never help but are hard to ignore. Even now I sometimes fall back into questioning my priorities and myself. Spending time writing this book often makes me uncomfortable when I think of what else I could be doing.

The following is taken from 8/16/2014 and my Morning Pages, a practice of stream-of-consciousness writing that I was doing each morning, as described in Julia Cameron's book *The Artist's Way*. Curt was 44 and had been living away from home for 28 years.

> *Yesterday afternoon Curt didn't want to go to his home*
> *[the group home where he'd lived for twenty-two years.]*
> *He literally pushed me back out of his doorway and*
> *walked to my car. I rolled my eyes at Tony [staff] and*
> *decided to spend more time, letting him sit in the car*
> *in the driveway while I visited with a friend on my cell*
> *phone. Curt seemed happy in the car and didn't com-*
> *plain a half hour later when we tried again to go back*
> *to his house. He got out of the car and walked up to the*
> *entryway but stopped at the doorway. Even when Tony*

opened the door, Curt growled and didn't want to go in. Mention of eating, going to the bathroom, the normal things that get Curt back into his normal routine— nothing seemed to help. I had to have Tony hold Curt's hands as I retreated out the door, promising to see Curt again in two weeks.

Guess I haven't seen him frequently enough lately. I now live almost three hours away in another state. Actually, I was planning on spending time next week visiting friends nearby and will go early to see Curt, so it won't be long before I see him again. But I still feel bad.

I feel guilty because I've been spending a lot of time with Laura and her family and taking time for myself. I know Curt is fine and has a good life, but his show of defiance makes me feel bad. I know he has a mind of his own and clearly expresses what he wants and doesn't want. It's just very hard to see him reach for me and to have to say, 'no.' I was shortening our visit because I wanted to go pick out some artwork to put in this book. Is that more important? Is my selfishness, my taking care of myself, this book, more important? Was it just because I have been thinking so much about how independent he is and how many times I have chosen to nurture his independence? Because I want illustrations for my book?

It's not without pain, not without poignant reminders that he does not lead 'a normal' life and is restricted greatly compared to other young men in their 40s ... but they would be tied down to jobs, to family of their own, to their problems. So, I drove home without a radio to distract me, with only the relief of these

Morning Pages ... Mourning Pages.

*No amount of guilt can change the past. No amount of
anxiety can change the future.*

~Umar Ign al-Khattab

But feeling guilty doesn't help Curt or me. Neither does
worrying.

[From Morning Pages in 2013]

*Curt doesn't worry about weather or pine trees falling
on his head even though, during that flash tornado
several years ago, a fat pine fell next to his window.
Does he worry about anything? I don't think so. Does
he have the full range of emotions? I'm sure he does.
He must wonder where his favorite people are and
why someone who cares for him is there sometimes
but not forever. Bet he misses family but gets caught
up with the others who care for him and just goes on.
When he's hurting, he just folds up, pulls the covers
over his head and goes to sleep. That's the way I felt
this morning. It was a combination of delight in listening to the rainfall on the new metal roof and a deep,
confusing, pervasive sadness. What do I want that
I don't have? Why am I letting anything prevent me
from happiness?*

I'll always wonder: if I had been more assertive those first 10 days of Curt's life, would I have made his life easier? His chromosome disorder was there from the moment of conception, but I'm sure it didn't help him to get so dehydrated after his birth. Isn't that worrying about something that does not serve my well-being and is a totally useless waste of my energy? When I feel like that, it's time to get up, make hot tea, and function. A gratitude list—that always sits on my kitchen table—also changes my attitude. A book that has been inspirational for me and helpful in balancing my intense emotions is Michael Singer's *The Untethered Soul, the Journey Beyond Yourself.*

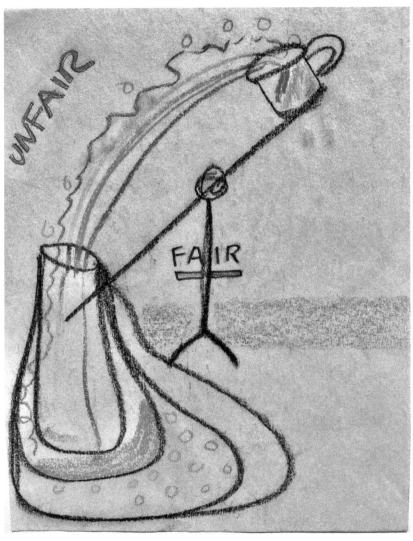

"Unfair"

Expressing Emotions in a Healthy Way

Richard Engel and his wife went public in 2018, expressing their frustrations and hopes after the birth of their son who was diagnosed with Rett Syndrome, a genetic brain disorder usually found in females. Engel has covered wars for years as an NBC correspondent, so he likened their response as parents to that of Post-Traumatic Stress Disorder. He has a website and an interview is available online, but his two premises are that being mentally strong is imperative, and the best way to do that is to talk about your feelings. He also states that isolation is not good for mental health. His interview and dedication are powerful, and you won't have to understand the impact of being in a war to understand his feelings. I agree with his recommendations.

My mother was an artist and unconsciously understood the power of art to express emotions. She helped me out practically, but I don't remember any advice she gave me about parenting. However, she did do something that changed the balance in my life. When Curt was about six months old, my mother signed me up for a printmaking course at a local museum school. She announced it to me and told me that while I was in class, she'd watch the baby. Creating art focused my emotions. Anger, confusion, and feeling that life was unfair were emotions I could draw on paper even when I could not talk about them. Making images also helped me remember that I indeed was someone besides a parent. Making art was something I could do to create beauty and to have control over something. That was the beginning of my understanding of art as therapy.

Personal writing works. Writing connects me to myself, my ideas, my greater, better self, and also my fearful, whiny, narpy self. Writing helps me see beyond the small stuff to the larger picture. Writing is self-therapy, mind clearing, and centering.

It gets me to put stuff clearly on a white page in words, just as making art gets images on paper. Anger, hurt, or fear can be expressed and dealt with safely on paper. Writing organizes and frames my thoughts. Writing by oneself is cheap, quick, easy, and almost equipment free. Writing with others has even more benefits. Art, singing, and writing are my modes of expression. You will find yours; it may be baking, crocheting, gardening, sewing, anything creative to nurture yourself, even if it's only for an hour a week.

Why write about Curt? It's one of my life challenges. Of course, the ultimate lesson is that I can't control his life or anyone else's, but in this earthly life he was born from me, and I am his mother—a link that lasts forever. These thoughts are shared because so many other people have similar situations. Having a child with disabilities is one category of life's challenges that is recognizable, has been around as long as humans have been, and will continue to be a challenge for future mothers. Nevertheless, it's not that different from other life challenges that each of us faces. Caring for any other individual can be much the same. The reasons why that person is in need of care vary, and the length of time the caring is necessary differs, but the stresses and joys are similar, so I believe my experience is worth writing about and reading about. We all can learn from one another and identify with others. It helps to know we are not alone in our experiences. It also helps to get some good, practical advice! I do know very well that we human beings frequently ask for advice, but we only take it if it "seems right" or "strikes a chord." Take everything I say with a grain of salt, and use what makes sense to you to make each day one of joy and connection with all the very special people around you.

Sleep and Food

How different it is to wake up bright or drowsy! The complete joy of waking after a full, deep sleep becomes a treasure and is rarely experienced once you become a parent. When Curt was living at home, nights were unfortunately predictable. Probably because of the anticonvulsant drug Phenobarbital, Curt slept about two hours at a time during the night. He would wake up and play most of the time, but I could hear him, even though our bedroom was upstairs and his downstairs. He didn't know how to pull covers over his body, and the house was always cold at night, so after he'd make his little, happy hollering noises for a while, he'd get cold and start to cry. He had a bladder like a camel and only urinated a few times a day or night, but when he did ... It happened often enough that changing the bedcovers in the middle of the night and getting him changed into dry pajamas and warmed up again became routine.

Does that sound awful? In some ways it was because I was in a constant state of fatigue, but it was actually heart expanding. Recently, I read Maria Mutch's beautifully written book, *Know the Night, A Memoir*, that describes the way she coped with long nights with her son; the book reminded me of those years of Curt's awakening during the night. Curt was always delighted to see me at any hour. He smiled and laughed and flapped his arms. As soon as he could, he would jump up and down, hold onto the crib railings, and chant, "Ma-MAH, Ma-Mah, Ma-MAH" over and over again. I would rock him in the rocker and sing lullabies to him softly until he fell asleep again, his thick dark lashes reluctantly closing over his eyes like a stage curtain at the end of the show. I'd trudge back up the stairs, and he'd sleep for another two or three hours, then we'd repeat it all over again until the morning light and time to get the household up for school.

The only way I was able to get enough rest was by doing Transcendental Meditation at least once a day. It saved me—and the whole family—because, with 20 minutes of meditation in the afternoon, I was able to get deep rest equivalent to eight hours of sleep. Every day at 2:30 PM, I put the kids into their beds or room for quiet time, and I did my meditation, even if they were hollering for me. In truth, I know they both understood and welcomed the stillness. They got used to it and respected my need for the time off. My husband never seemed to remember and would call for me and be upset that I didn't answer when I was "medicating," as he feebly joked.

Food is as primary as sleep, and I didn't know much about nutrition when Curt was born. (Did you note the many references to Jell-O in my 1970 diary?) When I realized that getting him to eat and trying to keep him healthy was lifesaving, I started reading *Prevention* magazine and joined the nearby food co-op. Those were the days of earthy-crunchy meals and "back to the earth" projects. Both kids loved going to the co-op on Saturday mornings to pick up food and do their share of the chores to help out. Convinced that natural foods would benefit my family, I cooked with no white flour or white sugar.

We didn't know much about nutrition back then, but now we know that diet dramatically affects individuals with Down syndrome and that many on the autism spectrum have food allergies. There is a tremendous amount of information available online. Providing nutritious food for my family helped me balance my life too. A note of caution though: struggling to make everyone in the family eat healthy food, important as that is, should be balanced with other priorities. Be realistic and flexible. Mealtime shouldn't be a battleground.

"Super Lucy…there has got to be a better way"

Learning to be Assertive

In spite of the feminist movement that was gaining traction in the early 1970s, I found that speaking up and making myself heard wasn't easy, but I learned it was especially true when dealing with the medical world.

I've learned that the television dramas depicting urgent care aren't the realty of any emergency room we've ever visited. We had many, many visits to the ER to get Curt looked at when he hit his head or face when having a seizure. He has usually had good care, even though the wait to be seen averaged six to eight hours (and still does.) Curt has never lost consciousness from an impact and doesn't bleed very much. We wait and the doctor assesses whether he needs stitches. Curt hates bright light in his eyes, so examinations are difficult. I've learned to cover his eyes with a wet cloth and hold him as steady as I can while the doctor administers topical anesthetic. Once, when a doctor started to sew up a cut without any anesthetic, saying, "People like this don't feel any pain," I was furious as well as astonished and insisted upon something to ease the pain. I had to learn to be insistent, but I did learn.

Another time when I took Curt to the ER, I overheard the resident say to another, "There's nothing wrong with that patient except an overanxious mother." That infuriated me, but I refused to leave. A half hour later, Curt's pediatrician came to examine him and admitted him to the hospital.

There is an old saying: "You catch more flies with honey than with vinegar." Uncomfortable as I am with the thought that I consider myself manipulative enough to use "honey," it is nevertheless worth saying that the *way* you are assertive makes a huge difference in getting results. Being assertive does not mean being unpleasant or aggressive. A favorite helpful book is *Self Esteem* (2000) by McKay and Fanning, if you need coaching.

That brings up another reality that was very difficult for me. I tried to take care of everything myself. I wanted to be strong, but I didn't have enough medical knowledge to know when I should take Curt to the hospital or when to keep him at home and wait. Does he need stitches or not? Is he seriously dehydrated? Is he drug toxic? I tended to choose not to go for help when I probably should have. It was not a matter of whether or not to be assertive but a question of giving up responsibility when I was not able to make a decision. At one point, Curt's regular pediatrician took me aside and reminded me that I had another child at home and did not have to take care of my son all the time by myself. He told me that anytime I needed him to make the decision about hospitalization that I should just to let him know; he would make that decision for me, and I would not have to. After that, whenever I took Curt to his office, the doctor would first look at me and ask if I needed him to take the responsibility of decision-making. What a relief that was!

Taking Time for Yourself and Your Spouse

It is not heroic to never leave the side of your disabled child. Everyone needs time to be alone, to restore, to get away. Even you. Especially, you. Remember the "Martyr Mother Syndrome"? You will be a better parent if you take care of yourself, and that means going on vacation, having fun and laughing, and getting away by yourself as well as with your spouse and other children.

Being on vacation or away from home can be stimulating, exhausting, and disorienting, and so is returning from any time away. Most often Home Sweet Home is inviting upon return, and the familiar is comforting, but sometimes it's the return that wearies and worries. Being away can mean seeing the worn-out carpet, chipped paint, and sticky screen door with dismay or with a resolve to fix things or let them be, just like

Jimmy Stewart, who kisses the banister newel post that falls off in his hand at the end of the movie "It's a Wonderful Life!" Perspective and opportunity are gained from some distance, but it's also a time to count blessings, change what doesn't work, review, slow down, and start again.

Taking time to be with your partner or spouse on a regular basis is just as important as a big vacation. Getting away together, even for short periods of time, can strengthen the relationship when you use the time away to reconnect, share feelings, and remember why you love one another. In the many places I've researched statistics for divorce in marriages with a disabled child, the results are often conflicting but not encouraging, but that's the last thing you want to hear from me or research studies. Marriage is hard enough, and this is just an additional challenge. Your disabled child is one of many influences on a marriage. I do believe that it is extremely wise to take time to be with your spouse, express your emotions, and work out ways to support one another and love one another. In my two marriages, caring for Curt stressed one and strengthened the other, but having a child with disabilities was one of many factors that created stress.

Curt was our first child; we didn't have any system about parenting or sharing our emotions when he was born. However, we stayed together until it was time for Curt to leave home at age 16, and I know that getting away as a couple helped make that possible, and having a good night or two of uninterrupted sleep was wonderful. An added long-term bonus is that many who helped us get away ended up becoming physical therapists, teachers, and classroom aides.

Suspend Judgment of Others, Keep Learning

There have only been a handful of times that my son has ever acted like he was not glad to see me, and those times set off alarms about his health or drug levels. There has never been a time when he didn't know me. Sure, he calls other women "Mamah," but he always knows me. I wonder how it is with parents of children on the autism spectrum; how does it change things if a child is unable to relate? I also know that I have been wrong and judgmental about whether someone relates to me or not. I've always tried to speak to others assuming they understand and can respond to me. Unfortunately, I have sometimes judged unfairly and incorrectly and failed to recognize a person's unique humanity.

[Written as a memory on 12/7/15]

Years ago, when Curt was in elementary school and under the legal requirements of Chapter #766 in MA that says he was entitled to education in the "least restrictive environment" possible, he was placed in a completely separate school. It was actually a former school then used just for storage, except for the one room that housed the classroom. One room was cleared and a table with chairs around it was their school space. I don't remember a window; the place was gray everywhere. It had been Pleasantview School before it was mothballed, but there wasn't anything pleasant about it. I was outraged!
I called a special meeting and was told that my son was "not responding" and that Pleasantview was the best place they could find for him. I remember getting

very angry and raising my voice, saying, "He is not responding because the place is grim, there is no stimulation or light!" The supervisor said, "Curt does not respond to the others in his class," and I retorted cruelly, "There is nobody home there! Nobody can even move independently, much less talk. Why would Curt be responsive to other individuals like that?" Eventually, the entire class was moved to a school with other children, but my judgment of the other individuals in his class is a memory I am ashamed of. Ironically, one of the individuals in that unstimulating classroom has pretty much followed Curt his whole life and has been a housemate for over 20 years now. This individual has no voluntary movement as far as I can tell; he does not make eye contact, cannot sit alone, and is fed via a gastro-intestinal tube. We'll call him Karl. In my mind I have always felt like he isn't really present, but my son, Curt, knows otherwise.

Not long after Curt moved to his current residence, he and I went shopping before Valentine's Day, and I picked out a box of chocolates for his house staff. When we got back from shopping, we paused at the front door; I coached him, "When the door opens, give Donna the candy, and we'll say Happy Valentine's Day!" Curt can't say anything like that, of course, but that's the way I talk to him. The door opened, Curt looked at Donna, whom he adores. He smiled, held onto the candy, walked right past her and into Karl's room, where he put the box of candy next to Karl in his bed. So much for my perception of who needed a treat! Probably twenty years later, Karl was still in our

lives, and I had never heard him make a sound. A few
years ago, when Karl and Curt were vacationing at
my house, I was visiting with one of my favorite staff
members, and Karl was in his hospital bed nearby.
The TV was blasting with a pro football game where
Karl could see it. I hate the use of TV for "companion-
ship noise" and don't follow sports at all, so I was a
bit annoyed at the noise. All of a sudden Karl started
laughing loudly and deeply and flapping his hands.
The staff person just smiled and said, "Oh, Karl's just
excited. His favorite team just scored a touchdown!"
I was flabbergasted and felt judgmental and hyp-
ocritical. For years I had believed that Karl was
unresponsive! I have to constantly remind myself
to see each individual as whole and complete and
worthy. If I can't do it, I certainly can't expect it of
others. And I'm so grateful that my son lives with
people who talk to everyone as if he or she gets it and
is really "in there."

Knowing Curt knows me and other family members doesn't
mean that we, his nuclear family, are the only ones he cares
about or care about him. He's lived away from home now
longer than he lived at home. Being loved or cared about
doesn't shrink one's capacity to love; it expands it. Saying and
showing love helps it grow. Many times when Curt and I are
together, I get frustrated with his behavior or angry about
his choices, but I still love him and he knows it. He can't talk,
but even when the time comes when he is no longer able to
respond, or when the time comes that I am unable to respond,
"I love you, too, Curt," I will always love being his mother.

All About Attitude and the Attic

The problem is not the problem.
The problem is your attitude about the problem.

~Captain Jack Sparrow

When we understand that there are some things we can *do* to make our lives better but that *how* we do them is the key then this journey becomes peaceful or at least possible. A wonderful therapist used a simple metaphor that has helped me many times when confronted with the choice—and my attitude—about doing or not doing something. She used the example of cleaning or not cleaning the attic:

You have four choices:

- You can clean the attic in distress.
- You can clean the attic peacefully.
- You can not clean the attic in distress.
- You can not clean the attic peacefully.

It's not about *doing* anything; it's about *being* and your attitude. With the birth of your child with disabilities, you have been given a marvelous teacher, and you can control your attitude.

Take Care of Your Spirit, Soul: Develop a Sense of the Meaning of Life

The only advice I remember my father giving me about parenting was, "Join a church. You'll need it." That made me upset at first because I thought he meant that, because we all thought Curt would die, I would need a place for the funeral service. That's not what he meant, and his advice was sound. It doesn't matter if you go to a church, synagogue, a spiritual book group, or mosque. It's very satisfying to spend at least an hour a week experiencing being cared for and hearing words to affirm that there is, indeed, meaning to life. Look around, visit places, but choose an organization that affirms your worth and believes that all people—even those who will never be able to sit up, learn to read, or have a real job—are valued and loved. A worthy organization/religion is a community that will support you just because you belong, and that makes a world of difference. Don't do this alone. You don't have to. Let others support you.

> *Choose people who lift you up.*
>
> ~Michelle Obama

And while you're doing all this, perhaps you'll start to understand and give meaning to the joys and sorrows you experience. Take time to wonder about it. Ask questions. Listen to wise ones. Read. Watch meaningful movies and videos. (See a list of some of my favorite movies under References/ Inspiration.) Don't waste time and energy on negativity or with negative people; they can be toxic. Clean out the attic or don't go near it, but do it with love and optimism. Take care of yourself, develop or embrace some practice or belief system that helps you make sense of life. It's all about balance, whether you have one or two legs. Try to balance your mind, body, and spirit.

> *Life is all about balance. Since I only have one leg, I understand that well.*
>
> ~Sandy Fussell, *Shaolin Tiger*

CHAPTER 2

Your Child

*This chapter focuses on the uniqueness of your child,
specific needs, personality, and the joy and difficulty of
seeing him or her past the diagnosis and prognosis.*

"Mother, Child, Spirit"

Diagnosis

Your child may have a well-documented disability, or doctors and teachers may spend years trying to figure out "what is wrong." Although we had a diagnosis early on, there were no others to compare with due to the rarity of Curt's condition, so we just learned as he grew. Nevertheless, no matter what the diagnosis, your child is unique, different from all other individuals who ever inhabited this earth. He may be the product of combined genetic material from you and your partner or totally unrelated to you biologically, but his genetic material came from two distinct people and formed a unique person.

After Curt's initial difficult month, he regained his birth weight and started to put on pounds because I'd switched to bottle feeding and could monitor his intake. When he was stabilized, our pediatricians gave an initial diagnosis and told us to institutionalize him for the short time he was expected to live. In my parents' time, institutionalization was commonly chosen, but it was 1970, just several years before Federal laws were passed to give children with disabilities the right to education, and the state schools for "the retarded" were still full. The times were to change even though his pediatricians may not have known that. However, we never even considered institutionalizing our child. Of course we didn't know how difficult keeping him at home would be.

Fortunately, the pediatricians suggested a second option. They suggested we go to a genetic specialist in Boston to confirm their diagnosis. That first diagnosis was wrong, and Curt got a second diagnosis about six weeks into his life. (See Chapter 4. OTHERS.) The diagnosis was a rare, partial deletion of a chromosome in the 13-15 group; there was one known case in Russia and one in Italy. Fortunately, along with the diagnosis, we got a brilliant and compassionate genetic specialist who would follow our son until he became an adult.

Don't believe everything the doctors/teachers tell you. Ask questions and get a second opinion and/or counsel from alternative sources. In the early years with Curt's diagnosis, there was little or no information for me about what the future would bring, but the current electronic age has connected people all over the world, so more information is now available than ever before. Keep looking, asking, and contributing information.

For me in those pivotal, early weeks, that lack of information was a gift because I could hope for anything and everything for my son. If Curt had Down syndrome, autism, blindness, or another better-documented disability, I would have had more information and other parents for support, but even within those diagnoses there is tremendous variation from person to person. I just had to let Curt be Curt and try to love him without expectations but at the same time encourage him to be the best he could be.

Uniqueness

I recently rediscovered notes written to Curt's primary care pediatrician from Dr. F., the genetics specialist we saw yearly. They describe Curt's development, and it's a good record, the best one I have from those early years, because it was a time when a patient's clinical notes weren't available as they are now. As I read through the comparisons of his development to "normal" development, I noticed one paragraph, dated 12/21/1971, when Curt was 18 months old:

> *His development has shown significant progress since he is now able to get to a sitting position and hold his bottle. His personality has also developed with some obstinate characteristics reflected in apparent developmental regressions such as refusing to feed himself.*

So, from early on, Curt's personality came through even in serious, factual medical records. I love it. In his entire life, people who get to know Curt describe him as "funny," "smart," "foxy," "a hoot!" Our first nickname for him was "Rascal." I have never called him "My Baby," "Poor Thing," "My Angel Child" or "My Gift from Heaven," because those terms just don't fit. He has never seemed pitiful or particularly angelic. He's mischievous, manipulative, and has an incredible sense of humor. In my 50 years of experience with individuals with various disabilities of all kinds, it seems to me that some of the most severely disabled individuals are some of the cleverest and most skillful in getting their needs met, probably because they have to work so hard at it. Curt uses his very well-developed personality and seems to be able to charm people. He's particularly fond of attractive women, loves older women with white hair—who probably remind him of his loving grandmother—and adores being with other guys who treat him like a guy. His caregivers often call him "Bubba," and he has nicknames for his favorites. He has always been a great judge of character and will seek the attention of those who will like him. He rarely goes to anyone who does not like him or who ignores him.

Your child with disabilities will have physical and personality traits from both sides of the family, just as any other child does. He may have his father's thick, curly hair, his mother's love of spicy food, or Uncle Joe's deep voice. Enjoy these gifts of genetics, as you do with other family members, and you'll notice that others do too. Focus on the similarities rather than the differences, the strengths as well as the weaknesses. Then think of what unique gifts your child has and what he has come into your life to teach you as often as you think of what gifts you have to be able to teach your child. Be inspired by this quote from among the most well-known and remarkable individuals with disabilities:

My advice to other disabled people would be, concentrate on things your disability doesn't prevent you going well, and don't regret the things it interferes with. Don't be disabled in spirit as well as physically.

~Stephen Hawkings

Wherever he went to school or camp, Curt was well liked and seemed to know how to find people who would be kind and loving. My son has a particular gift of being able to sense and seek out others who will respond positively to him. There have been only two times in his life when he strongly refused to go somewhere, didn't even want to get out of the car. Both times I over-ruled him and was proven wrong in doing that. Once, when he was young and enjoying various camps, we tried a new camp in Maine. When we got there, Curt refused to get out of the car. We insisted and left him there, knowing he was unhappy. The next morning we got a call: the camp was closing and we were to immediately come pick up our child. We should have paid more attention to Curt's instinctual reaction. The second time that happened was several years ago, and we spent months trying to figure out what was wrong. After failing to figure it out, we just decided that he needed a change, so we moved him from one program—where he refused to get out of the bus to enter—to another. We never figured out what was wrong or what he didn't like about the first program, but he still refuses to go there. I trust his instincts now.

My son has a unique personality and clearly is intelligent in certain ways. Gardner's book *Multiple Intelligences,* a book that describes eight different ways every person can show intelligence, is a classic that always reminds me that my favorite way of being intelligent—school smarts—is only one of several ways and that my son has interpersonal intelligence that serves him well. PS: I am still trying to learn to appreciate country music, a taste Curt has developed since living away from home, where I always listened to classical music.

When you focus on someone's disability, you'll over-look their abilities, beauty and uniqueness. Once you learn to accept and love them for who they are, you subconsciously learn to love yourself unconditionally.

~Yvonne Pierre, *The Day My Soul Cried: A Memoir*

Staying Alive and Staying Alert

Firstly, you will have to do what you can to keep your child alive and well. That task could take all your energy, time, and sanity. Unfortunately, you could lose yourself, your partner, your family, and maybe even your child, no matter how hard you try. Learning to balance keeping your child alive and keeping yourself and other members of your family functioning is a monumental juggling act. Most of us are not prepared for it. There is a good reason why the chapter on YOU is before this chapter on YOUR CHILD. Did you skip to this chapter? If you did, please go back to Chapter 1. YOU. When you learn to take care of yourself, you will be able to do what is necessary to take care of your child or get help to do so. Please be smarter than I was, and take care of yourself before your body, mind, or spirit is too exhausted or damaged to care for anyone.

An aspect of Curt's diagnosis that took me a while to understand was "failure to thrive." That accurately describes what happened soon after his birth, and it has been a common problem throughout his life, probably the most difficult challenge. It's a medical term, and I've always considered it a euphemism, but it's reality. When he was first born, he failed to thrive because he didn't have the instinct to suck. As he grew, he learned not only to eat but also to love to eat. Nonetheless, he still refuses to eat or drink whenever he is sick or doesn't feel well. A virus or sore throat can still cause him to shut down, but most often it has been a combination of some minor ailment and being drug toxic—having too much anticonvulsant medication in his blood, which causes grogginess, sleeplessness or sleepiness, slowed thinking, and a "drugged" feeling. Here is a passage I wrote about one of the many times this term manifested in our unique and stubborn young son.

[Written 9/2/14 about an event when Curt was about 10 years old.]

How many celebrations center on food! We certainly are a "food is love" family, and that's probably why my son's diagnosis of "failure to thrive" has had such emotional as well as physical consequences.
When Curt was about 10 years old, he got a virus and stopped eating or drinking. He was hospitalized, put on an IV, so he was out of danger from dehydration. He was there about 10 days, refusing to eat, when the doctor told me, "If he isn't eating by Monday, we'll put him on a feeding tube." It was Friday. That was not okay with me, so I got Curt discharged against the doctor's orders.
Normally, I fed my family health food: no white sugar or flour. However, this was a desperate situation. When their father took the kids out, he treated them to junk food, and they loved it, so from the hospital we went to the drive-thru at Burger King. Curt was in the back seat on the left side. I ordered burgers and fries, parked in the lot, moved into the back seat next to him, and set the food on the seat between us. The aroma of the sizzling meat started to fill the van; the smell

seemed to coat the upholstery.

I didn't offer Curt any food, because I had been begging him to eat for over a week. I just sat there, slowly chewing and listening to the car radio tuned to his favorite station. I sang; I slurped; I smacked my lips and hummed along. The cars whizzed by; the hamburger aroma floated around with the rock songs. Curt started to watch the cars; his happy noise returned. "No fries for you, Buddy," I warned him. "You have to go back and eat hospital food!" And I kept slurping. Eventually, he nabbed a French fry with his non-dominate right hand. I pretended not to see him gobble it down. (He has always been very skilled at stealing food.) Slowly at first, then with enthusiasm, he finished off the rest of the fries and burger. When I asked, "Want some Coke?" he laughed and grabbed the plastic cup. It was a celebration meal, one of the best kinds.

Years later, when he was in his teens, a similar situation occurred when he lived at a residential school away from home. He caught a virus, stopped eating and drinking, and was hospitalized. Again, I got him discharged from the sterile, metallic, impersonal environment of the hospital and returned to his loving group home, where his friends awaited. I'd told the staff about his previous experiences and the incident with the fries at Burger King and instructed them to pretend that nothing was unusual but to just sit him at the group table and let him decide when to eat. I'd just gotten home from dropping him off when the phone rang. I picked it up and heard, "One meatball!" and knew he would again be all right.

Here's another example of how my life was a balancing act. Every medical decision for Curt after he had his first seizure at six months old involved taking anticonvulsant medication. All medications have consequences, serious consequences. They can damage organs and cause drowsiness or irritably. Being over-medicated by drugs used to try to control his seizures has always been a major problem; it slowed his development and his ability to learn, communicate, and live a full life. Balancing the risk of injury from seizures and his alertness has been very difficult. I have always chosen to use the least medication advisable that would help control the seizures but not put him totally out of it. That has meant he has had many trips to the ER. His head and face are covered with scars from injuries incurred by his many-times-daily jack knife seizures.

In my most recent disagreement with a medical person's prescription for Curt's medication, I was told, "When he has a seizure, they call me, not you" (which is not true.) I still choose to have Curt as clear minded as possible and suspect that in this case the medication was causing very negative side effects, as well as lethargy. I asked to be referred to the medical person's supervisor and, eventually, got the medication discontinued. Managing the medication levels was hard enough when he was living at home and his emergency care affected every member of the family. Since he's been living in a group home, I have had to factor in how horrible staff members feel when Curt gets hurt from having a seizure; consequently, he gets more medication than I wish but has fewer seizures.

Even now, at age 50, Curt will refuse to eat or drink when something is wrong or when he hurts. He must have lots of pain, but ever since childhood he seems to have a high tolerance for it. One of the most frustrating things about being with a basically non-verbal person is that person's inability to tell you what he thinks or feels. When a child screams in pain, a mother naturally says, "Where does it hurt? What's the matter?" When the pain is too great, the child is unable to answer but usually clutches the sore place, the bee string, or the scraped knee. Curt rarely does that. We taught him the sign for pain and use it to try to locate what's wrong, and that helps, but it's not always reliable. He is not able to tell us which part of his body hurts. He must have frequent headaches, probably has esophageal pain from acid reflux, and certainly had horrible pain from the hemorrhoids he had for years. As he has grown older, his pains are more pronounced, as are the stresses on his bones. He is now struggling to walk and uses a wheelchair at times. It's still a balance between keeping him safe and keeping him alert.

Your child will have different but unique medical and developmental challenges and successes, and they must be taken care of. What is needed are good observation skills to be able to report to your doctors and knowledge of your child's normal patterns of behavior. See Chapter 5. PRACTICAL for some suggestions about managing the physical care and recordkeeping, and Chapter 3. FAMILY for my thoughts on how to help your family, and Chapter 4. OTHERS to get help.

Living in the Moment, Living His Moment : The Power of Now

Having a child with a disability changes every aspect of life, so consider that some of these changes that seem like problems may have benefits. The challenges can become gifts. I'm not saying that raising a child with extra demands upon your time, energy, patience, money, and sanity is the best thing that will ever happen to you, but each moment, each day, you have the option of how you will feel about what you are doing, as well as what you actually do. Remember my therapist's advice about attitude and cleaning the attic? Attitude can make the ordinary seem extraordinary. Sometimes, the ebb and flow of life eventually absorbs the extraordinary, and it then becomes your ordinary.

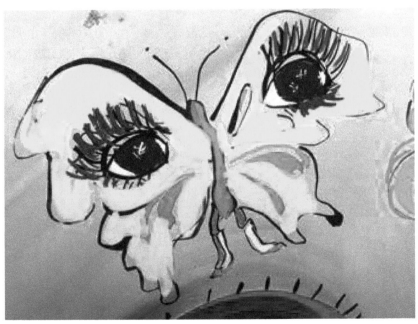

"Butterfly with Braces"

Learning to see and appreciate the unique patterns of behavior and choices your child presents to you will change your own patterns and way of looking at the world. Perhaps looking at the world through his eyes—no matter how well he can see—is a chance to learn something about the world you might not have wanted to see or didn't have time to notice. It will present you with many opportunities to change your expectations and teach you how to pay attention to little things—and big things such as time.

Sometimes, a friend or family member will help you see unique qualities of your child and remind you that his world will not be your world. This poem was written by a friend:

To Curtis
  on a rainy day
You are a Misty field of flowers,
Curt.
Somehow, one feels that there should be a switch
behind the right ear (like the jeweled steed
in the Arabian Nights' tale.)
You flick it on
And everything's in focus—words, eyes, limbs ...
But for now you're skywalking, Curt,
stumbling through clouds we can't focus on.
From the sound of your
laughter, tuned to unknown birds,
the sun's out there.
Curt, Curt,
boy with chocolate penny eyes!

~By Kay Campbell

Even now, when worries weigh me down, when the world news brings fear to my heart, or details of a British murder mystery I watched on TV keep me awake, I instinctively want to be with Curt. Even when he's had a time of unhappiness and distress, he is still the person I most want to be with to soothe my anxiety. Of course, I sometimes worry about him—my dreams of him are usually about his getting lost—but conversely, I don't worry much about him, because his core being is so present. He lives each moment for what it is. He certainly has a fine memory; he knows exactly where his favorite books are kept and where the refrigerator is! But he doesn't worry about the future or worry about what is next. He surely doesn't worry about money. Imagine that!

We must let go of the life we have planned, so as to accept the one that is waiting for us.
~Joseph Campbell

CHAPTER 3

Us: Family

"Family Gathering, Four Generations"

Being a Family

Balancing the physical and emotional needs of everyone in the family is challenging. Parent(s) and other children have their special needs too. Each one wants and deserves to "be seen," not ignored but cherished. Trying to have a normal, ordinary, family life requires good communication—family meetings?—and adjustments, but being a part of a family is natural and normal. Include your child whenever you can, but take time with your spouse and other children and other families.

Myth: People with disabilities are more comfortable with "their own kind."

Fact: In the past, grouping people with disabilities in separate schools and institutions reinforced this misconception. Today, many people with disabilities take advantage of new opportunities to join mainstream society.

Myth: The lives of people with disabilities are totally different than the lives of people without disabilities.

Fact: People with disabilities go to school, get married, work, have families, do laundry, grocery shop, laugh, cry, pay taxes, get angry, have prejudices, vote, plan, and dream like everyone else.

~Easterseals.com

Your child may have special needs, but he also has all the regular needs and delights of other children. That means he will thrive in a regular family environment and want to be a part of your family and be with other kids. When he gets older, he will enjoy having his own family if that is possible and experience living in the community. When my kids were young, we had an active family life with church friends, neighbors, and good friends who also had kids with whom we got together at least once a week. It was wonderful being able to socialize and have the children all be together. The adults would hang out in one area of the house, and kids would all get together and include Curt with them. Those dear friends made our family life very special and made growing up so much easier for both children. Those were times when Curt's disability melted into the love and acceptance of "normal" family life.

We did have other friends, neighbors, and family members who were not as comfortable with Curt as our "best" friends, but we always wanted to include Curt as much as possible. Perhaps it was unconscious, but we had a friend we actually spent regular time with who just seemed to ignore Curt. The man was an executive and held a responsible position in training and management at a local company, so I'm not sure why he didn't "get" Curt, but Curt did understand Dave, didn't like being ignored, and responded, perhaps a little impolitely:

[Written in 2015 around the time when Curt was about 12 years old]

I remember one time when we had a friend and his wife over for dinner. We all sat around the dining room table, with Dave at the head of the table and the adults at that end, the two children at the far end.

*I don't remember anything we had for dinner, but
we probably had some meat, some potatoes, salad,
and green beans. It was near the end of the meal,
and Dave had done most of the talking. I remember
thinking that it was time to clear the table and looked
around to see if everyone was finished with the meal.
Dave's plate was not empty, perhaps because he'd
been doing most of the talking. Just about that time,
Curt got up from the table and walked toward Dave.
He got next to him and just stood there watching him.
Dave kept talking and did not acknowledge Curt. Then
Curt reached out and picked up a green bean from
Dave's plate and pushed it into Dave's mouth!*

There are some people who will never understand your child and may never be able to relate to other people unlike themselves. We're all different, including those who do not include people other than themselves; just try to make the most of each situation.

Typical Family Stages

A "typical family" is an illusion, but there are natural, developmental stages that most families go through. Every family is different; every family is a composite of different beliefs, habits, cultural backgrounds, and personalities, from the traditional, two-parent family to extended families, two-mommy or two-daddy families, and single-parent homes. Each child in a family stirs up that mix with his own personality, individual needs, and preferences. Unfortunately, not everyone in your extended family will rally to help you; some may not agree with your choices, and a few will add stress to your already stressful situation. A child with disabilities naturally adds to this complex mix, but there is still a predictable pattern because parents/people raise babies who typically take about 18 years to grow into young adults.

Whether children are physically, emotionally, or intellectually "mature" at age 18 makes some difference, but 18 years is a natural time for the childhood stage of family life to be ending. The needs of children who cannot take care of themselves are different from those who can physically care for themselves but still need guidance to learn the tasks required to be able to live an independent life away from their parents. In most families, children grow up and move away to establish their own lives. A child with disabilities can throw off that natural pattern if he is never going to be able to take care of himself or live independently, but a disabled child of 18 may want to live independently or in an assisted-living situation away from home. As children move away from home and create their own worlds, parents take on new roles, perhaps becoming grandparents. In most cases, children usually outlive their parents. Parents of disabled children are very uncomfortable if they have not made arrangements for the care of their dependent children after they die.

I know that may be hard to hear if your child is fragile and/or developmentally young, but please consider this pattern as you make decisions about all the members of your family. Deciding to send my son to a residential school at age 16 was a very difficult decision, but once it was made, it became very clear it was the right decision for our family. Building up to that day were many years of a steady pattern of family life and an accumulation of daily choices that formed the foundation for the change.

Roots and Wings

One of my favorite sayings is, "There are only two lasting bequests we can hope to give our children. One of these ... is roots, the other, wings." (Hodding Carter, 1953.) Giving children the security to make them feel rooted in your love, acceptance, and support is a major job. Giving them education, guidance, and opportunities to develop physical and emotional maturity gives them the wings they will need to fly away from the family and establish their own lives. When one of your children is slower to develop, it doesn't mean that the process stops, it just slows down parts of it. A 20-year-old person who cannot feed or dress himself can be as emotionally independent as a person of so called "normal" functional abilities. There is no set pattern, but all families have cultural patterns about when children are "grown up" enough to go away to school, join the military, get married, etc. In the few articles currently available online when I searched "What do I need to know about raising a child with disabilities?" *every* one of them said to help your child become as independent as possible.

What is your family's pattern of expectations about independence? The family I grew up in was extremely liberal and lacked hard and fast rules. We were expected to be honest, smart, and do the right thing. "The right thing" wasn't written down or even talked about, but we all seemed to know what it was. Know the term "helicopter parent"? My mother never hovered at all; she was an artist and sometimes traveled overseas with my dad. I went away to Girl Scout camp early. My sister cried and never went to camp, but as a grown up, she travels more than the rest of us combined. My brother seems to have become independent early on. Somehow, we all managed to grow up without a lot of guidance, but we knew we were loved and smart enough to make decisions on our own. Learning independence is a matter of attitude as well as actions; no matter what your family values have been, your child with disabilities will benefit from as much independence as possible.

After my son survived his failure to thrive at birth, his father and I decided that we weren't going to let Curt's frailty keep us from traveling and doing what we wanted to do. At six weeks old, when he had regained his birth weight and seemed to be doing well, we went on a vacation for a week with him. We tried to act like a normal family from the beginning. I only knew what I had grown up with, but our family life was remarkably like that of our friends. My husband and I went out by ourselves and left the kids with sitters, mostly from our church. We paid the sitters reasonably, left them with lots of written instructions and a phone number, and dealt with problems if they arose. We had young couples who would move in for the weekend so we could go away as a couple. One couple loved to clean but didn't cook, so we would return to find the house spotless but a trash barrel full of take-out containers from Burger King and a local Chinese restaurant. Another couple loved to cook, so the kitchen was messy, but delicious leftovers awaited us in the refrigerator. The kids loved their sitters and looked forward to the change in routine and the energy of having young people play with them all weekend.

I sent Curt to camp when he was six. He had just learned to walk independently and actually ran most of the time. It was a wonderful special-needs camp run by the Rehabilitation Department of Boston University. I was working at a preschool for severely disabled and able-bodied children at the time, and two other mothers/friends who also worked at the preschool decided to try this camp along with me. We took a big station wagon with Curt and my friends' children, a boy who had spina bifida (a defect in the spinal cord) and a girl who had epidermolysis bullosa (a genetic skin condition). We three mothers were anxious, but the kids were excited. We got to the campsite and were met by vigorous, healthy, young BU students in T-shirts and shorts. The children were unloaded and immediately got a staff buddy. Curt's buddy was an attractive young blonde woman. I turned my back to get his sleeping and duffle bags and then couldn't find him. He had gone off with his buddy and never even said goodbye. He had a wonderful time. A week later, when I picked him up, he was flapping his hands and laughing, but he did greet me with a loud, "Ma-Mah!" All the counselors gathered around and cried to see the kids leave.

Balance in the Family

Curt and Laura with tire swing

MYTH: Non-disabled people are obligated to "take care of" people with disabilities.

FACT: Anyone may offer assistance, but most people with disabilities prefer to be responsible for themselves.

~Easterseals.com

Am I always balancing my attention between my children? When they were young, it clearly was Curt who took up most of my time. His younger sister, Laura, was aware of it and sometimes called me on it. On Saturdays their father paid attention to them; he would take turns going one-on-one to the dump and then to the donut place with each child, one per week. It was a careful Daddy time that we monitored and made sure the kids understood it was *equal time* with each of them, but the rest of the time it wasn't fair. There was no way around it. A kid with special needs takes more time—for many years, if not a lifetime. Their physical dependency is clearly a factor that no one can ignore, and certainly, your other children are well aware of it. Take time with your other children and do special things with them.

Caution: Separate physical dependency and emotional dependency. There is no reason to make your disabled child emotionally dependent upon you any more than your other children. Second caution: Do *not* make your other children the caretakers of your child with disabilities. Hire a sitter, trade for services with friends if you have to, but having to take care of a brother or sister all the time builds resentment. Helping out, everyone helping out, including your special needs child— you can think up ways for him to "help"—is key to family life. Rotating chores and being as fair as you can is preferable to making one child responsible for another. Give all the children chores and responsibilities.

When I was working, we had a sitter come each afternoon until I got home. Both kids had chores: laundry, cooking, and feeding animals. The sitter had to help Curt on his day to "do supper." She helped him put the chicken in the crockpot, load it up with stock, rice, veggies, and herbs, and then turn it on to "make supper." Laura learned simple recipes, also with the sitter's help, and didn't worry that her job was more intricate than his. Both got praise for making supper and helping Mom.

Same with laundry. It took Curt longer, and he needed many prompts, but he was actually pretty good at putting dirty clothes in the washer and transferring them to the dryer. (He always has liked to throw things!) Loading the dishwasher took him a lot of time, but he liked it and got pretty good at it. Note: adults seem to have difficulty being able to tell if the dishes in the dishwasher are clean or dirty, so don't expect your child with disabilities to be able to distinguish. (Reserve the skill of distinguishing dirty or clean for his adult life; childhood is difficult enough!)

Feeding our many animals was pretty easy, except that we had to build elaborate enclosures to keep the cats away from the fish and the gerbils. Curt was the only one in the family who could catch an escaped gerbil. The rest of us would race around trying to grasp the fast-moving little rodent, but Curt would just sit, flapping his hands, then quickly snatch one up by the tail! Assign chores, make a chart, be consistent and flexible.

As much as you try to make the obvious, physical aspects

of family life as fair and equitable as possible, the emotional impact of having one family member disrupt normal patterns lingers. Even these many years after Curt went to live at a group home, my time with my daughter is still interrupted by his needs. I know she is very aware of it, and it's natural for her to be resentful as well as very understanding. I found notes from a vacation with her. She and I had met at a lovely resort across the country to have a peaceful time together, but her brother's needs interrupted our peace and quiet:

[1/4/1996: Curt had been living away from home for 10 years, and Laura had graduated from college]

... slept 'till 11:30 and just decompressed all day. It's so good to be with Laura! My head seems clearer and yet my throat is still sore but ... tonight Curt's residence called. Curt is sick; 104.2 fever and dehydrated. They took him to the local urgent care and couldn't get an IV in, so they took him to the hospital ER, and we're waiting to hear now. I feel a clamp of fear over my chest. Talked to one of the night shift at his house. She said everyone's been sick, not to feel like I gave him my flu, but I do feel guilty and don't know what to do. They can take care of him. It'll take me a day to get back, but maybe I'll feel better if I did. I don't think he's really in danger unless it doesn't get better or if they can't get his meds into him. Hope they'll be honest with me and call ASAP. Guess Jorge's [staff] being with him is the best of all. He really cares about Curt, and Curt likes him. Curt hasn't really been sick since he's been living at his group home; they certainly are trained to

deal with severe med needs. Hope he gets better fast
though; if he feels like I did and won't take meds or
swallow, it's going to be hard. He's so stubborn. He's
got good reserves now though, fortunately.

Thankfully, Curt got better and I didn't have to go to him at that time, but the precious time my daughter and I had set aside to just be together was interrupted yet again. It's simply untrue to say that having a family member with disabilities does not affect the family. Sometimes, it makes the family strong; certainly, it stresses the family. We learn that everything is so precarious, so subjective, that it all can crumble in a minute, a call, a strong wind. How fragile we all are! Would it be easier on families if our children didn't have pain and struggles? That's unrealistic, but failing to acknowledge the extra stresses a child with disabilities causes is also unrealistic. Talk to your children, all of them. Have family meetings, go to a church, synagogue, or support group, get help from other family members, and keep the lines of communication open.

The End of Childhood and Leaving Home

We got through Curt's childhood with the help of family, dear friends, our church, good doctors, and good luck, but his needs changed as the years went by. For one, his seizure activity became worse. The time when children finish childhood and start becoming adults and moving away from home is a natural development of family life for children with disabilities, as well as those without them. At 18 a disabled individual may not be able to talk, walk, or know the danger of nuclear power, but he is not a "child" or "baby," simply a person who has lived 18 years. I firmly believe that even though his body may be smaller than average, or his IQ low, that individual should be treated like an adult. No one wants to be treated like a baby, disregarded, teased, ignored, or isolated.

Following is writing from what I called "The Most Difficult Time of My Life." I hadn't learned yet to take care of myself very well, and my body was unable to continue caring for Curt well enough to keep him safe. I was emotionally drained. It was time for a change in our family.

[Written about the time Curt was 16 years old]
1986, a Pivotal Year

In 1986 Laura was 14 years old, beautiful and healthy, taller than I, and active in the band, swim team, and her church activities. Curt was 16 years old, about 85 lbs., small for his age, ambulatory, communicating with sign language, some sounds and gestures. His school placement was a separate classroom but in a noisy junior high school nearby; he loved riding the bus and had an afterschool paid companion who enjoyed being with him. Both were happy, quite independent, well-adjusted kids, but both were aware of mounting tenseness and bickering between their father and me. Curt would sometimes have seizures when his father and I were disagreeing; his sister spent more time with her new church friends.
I was a physical mess. The tension in the marriage and caring for Curt went into my neck, shoulders and jaw, so my TMJ (severe jaw pain) was horrible. Even a gentle touch on my cheek hurt; my mouth could barely open. My muscles hurt everywhere. Curt's seizures had recently changed and developed into a different pattern that I called "Series Seizures." They actually weren't as dangerous as his previous ones,

which came on without warning and jack knifed his
body to the left side. Those violent, jack-knifing ones
he'd had since early childhood meant that his face and
head were covered with scars from past falls. This new
pattern caused other risks and difficulties. With the
Series Seizures he would very slowly drop to the left
side and end up on the floor in a right angle for about
a minute; then he'd wake up, laugh, get up again, and
continue walking, running or whatever he was doing
for about a minute, and then a seizure would start all
over again. Sometimes, the Series Seizures lasted for
5 minutes. At the time I had no PRN (a prescription
to be given as needed to stop seizures) or anything I
could do to stop them. When he was having a seizure,
I couldn't pick him up or move him. He wasn't that
big, but I wasn't strong enough. One time it happened
crossing the street, and I thought we weren't going
to be able to get to safety. It was very stressful and
seemed to be the last straw. I just couldn't do it all. It
was the hardest decision of my life. Our family needed
restructuring, rebalancing, and we were all ready for
a change.
At the IEP (Individualized Educational Program) in
May, I sat at a table surrounded by Curt's teacher,
the Special Education Director (SPED), the Speech
Pathologist, the Occupational Therapist, the Physical
Therapist, Curt, Curt's father, and piles of papers and
reports from the neurologist and doctors. The SPED
Director started to outline the proposed plan for the
coming year involving the large support team assem-
bled in the room. I had to stop the proceedings and

*say, "I can't do this anymore. I hurt too much. I can't
keep him from danger, and I need help. I can't care
for my child any longer." I remember looking around
the room, feeling like a terrible mom but knowing it
was the best thing to do for my whole family. It was
suddenly very, very quiet for what seemed like a long
time. Then with efficiency and grace, the assembled
group changed course and started to plan for my son's
transition to a residential facility.*

The transition was actually quite easy. In September Curt
enrolled in a marvelous school for children with developmental
disabilities about an hour and a half away from our home.
He had been going to summer camps for 10 years, and we
had frequently left the kids with sitters, so he was used to
being away from home. He moved into the residential facility
comfortably and showed no signs of being homesick; he thrived
in his new environment. The staff was young, enthusiastic, and
immediately delighted with my funny, engaging little man. He
lived there and went to their school during the weekdays but
was required to be at home four days each month. Only once
did he cling to me for a few minutes when I dropped him off—
until his favorite staff person caught his attention! Curt was
emotionally ready and able to be in his own realm. He made
a peer friend for the first and only time in his life, gained 20
pounds, and grew six inches in the first year of this life—eating
white flour and sugar!

Curt's father and I divorced six months later, and my
daughter and I developed a new relationship with roots deep
and strong. The core of our divorce agreement was to equally
share the responsibilities of parenting Curt. It took quite a bit
of education, patience, me letting go, and time for his father
to "learn the ropes," but Curt's relationship with his father

changed and improved as they spent more time together.

   The whole experience was very similar to having a child enlist in the military, go to college, or move for a job. As difficult as the decision was for me, it was a natural one for any family. There were four of us, and we needed to change the dynamics in order to foster the growth of all of us. It was years before I slept through the night. It took 30 years before my stressed-out teeth got fixed and I could move my jaw comfortably. My hands still tingle and freeze when I hear a sound like that of a head hitting the table, but we are all healthier and happy. Curt's world is expansive; he's had structure that I was unable to provide and lots of fascinating people involved in his life that he would never have met if he'd stayed at home. The rest of us have changed and learned that love needn't be quantified or restricted to one's family. In the years since Curt moved away from home, his sister went off to college, spent years working in Europe, and started her own family. I went back to school, started a new career as an Art Therapist, and eventually remarried and inherited three stepchildren—and then grandchildren—who became a major part of my life and Curtis'.

"Curt and Step-Dad"

Adult Life, Aging

It changes, the finger on the pulse of life. For me the constant vigilance was over when Curt moved away from home. Occasionally, calls from the nurse where he lives cause my heart to flip and fingertips to tingle. Fortunately, staff learned to start each call with "Curt will be all right but ..."

Curt is still living in a group home at 50. The calls come only during the day; the staff doesn't wake me for an ER visit if he seems to be all right but is just being taken in because he hit his head during a seizure. They would rather be safe than sorry and are legally required to take him in to check, but so far they have not called me in the middle of the night. Some night, they may. At this writing, he is being quarantined in his group home because of the Covid-19 virus; everyone is monitored, temperatures checked, and precautions taken. He is getting the best care available, but I can't visit him.

Several years ago, when he was 44, Curt had a hard year of ups and downs with health and emotions. His temperament changed, and none of us knew what was going on. He bit his thumb in agitation until it was red and calloused. No one mentioned it at his annual ISP in April; it was a true elephant in the room. No one wanted to say that he had been unhappy, difficult to be with, disinterested, and withdrawn, because we all think of him as funny, engaged, and delighted in life.

As we walked out of the meeting, these disturbing changes were finally brought up. Immediately, the team got together, ordered tests, assessments, changes in medication, and suggested a change in his daily program. He was taking a medication we suspected affected him physically and emotionally, so he was weaned off it. He did change day programs, but it took over a year to make the changes and see improved results. He is better now, but the reality is that at 50 his body is old from years of heavy-duty medication. Each medication has warnings of damage to kidneys, liver, heart, etc. His bones are stressed and he struggles now to walk. My fingers ache from arthritis and years of him gripping them tightly to balance ... As we both age, I can imagine how he must feel.

I've had to reassess how I can be with Curt as we both grow older. I don't have the strength I used to have. He now outweighs me by 20 pounds and is much stronger, although unsteady on his feet. He frequently uses a wheelchair, and it does help me too. I'm now divorced again and greatly miss the loving, physical support Curt's stepdad provided, yet I know I can still count on his help when I need it. Nevertheless, I need to plan on doing most things alone. Depending upon others is more important now than ever. "Our world seems to have changed again in 2020, as many of my memories reflect different times. We adjust."

[Written 7/16. Curt was 46]

I never expected that Curt would live to be this old. Every day when he was a child, I would wake up wondering if he was alive and rush down to feel his nose for breathing if he was asleep. When he was older, he would wake me with his happy hollering, so I knew he was OK and wish for just a few more minutes of sleep. Now when he is visiting me, and I'm back "on duty," I sleep fitfully and anticipate getting up to give him his 6 AM medications. I sleep in the same room with one ear attentive to his sounds and dreading the labored, heavy breathing and clacking of teeth that indicate he's having a grand mal seizure. When I take him back to his home, I am always tired, relieved but glad of the time spent together. Sometimes, he is more comfortable visiting than others. Sometimes, he just wants to be in the car and sit there, and sometimes, he clearly wants to go "home" to his own house. Yesterday, I talked to Curt's house manager and started the process of having staff bring Curt and one or two of his housemates up to my New Hampshire home for a mini vacation. It didn't even occur to me that they would do it and take care of Curt at night, dress him, etc. while I stay comfy and calm in another room. I hope it works out and that it could become a pattern for the future when I no longer have the energy to bring Curt up here on my own.

It's easier now to see him for short times. I drive almost three hours to his house. Usually, we go to eat at Boston Market, where we can get mushy food like mashed potatoes and creamed spinach that can pass for pureed, since that is what he needs now. The staff there always greets us with enthusiasm and makes us feel at home. Every time we go there, someone helps with the heavy double doors; often it's another customer. It seems that just going at his pace and not expecting much is fine. Consequently, we spend time running errands or simply parking at a busy intersection where he can watch the cars and trucks go by. He has a portable wheelchair that I can still manage to get into the trunk of my car.

Recently, I have been trying to take Curt swimming at his local YMCA on Saturday mornings. Having the staff get his bathing suit on before I pick him up helps, as does using the wheelchair. I fought so hard to keep him out of a wheelchair, but honestly, it makes it easier for me to take him places now. Every single time we've gone swimming, we have made friends with someone in the pool. One time when Curt had a seizure in the locker room after swimming, a man we'd befriended in the pool literally caught Curt as he seized. "Tonic-clonic?" the man quickly asked. (Tonic-clonic is a medical term for a type of seizure that the average person usually doesn't know. It used to be called a grand mal seizure.) The man was a doctor but had not mentioned it when we were chatting in the swimming pool.

As patterns change, I find I need to let go of more of my expectations but find that it is liberating for me and probably for my whole family:

[Written 1/14/16]

Christmas 2016 was the first that I'd not been with Curt for Christmas in 46 years. Each year his interest in the holiday has diminished, but I was not able to accept it until last year. When the kids were both at home, we would make an expedition every year into the woods to cut down a tree. We'd pull Curt on a sled and go into the woods, cut down a tree, then pull the tree and Curt back out again and take it home on the roof of the car. Before we could get the kids out of their wet snowsuits, Curt would begin, "Light, light, light," until we got the lights strung up on the still-wet tree and watch as the heat of the lights melted the remaining snow and water collected on the carpet. One year we decided to hire a sitter and go out and buy a tree from the Boy Scouts in town. We brought the tree back and hid it on the back porch, planning to decorate it the following night. Next morning Curt got up, pulled the porch curtains back, discovered the tree, and started saying, "Light, light, light!" before breakfast. Because he loved the lights on the tree, he also insisted

that they be lit all the time, repeating, "Light, light!"
and signing until I crawled under the branches and
plugged them in. He loved outdoor lights as well. We'd
drive around the neighborhoods known for their dis-
plays. He'd point out the window, holler with delight,
and shout, "Light." Now he barely notices the lights
and just wants to drive around, especially at night.

Now, Curt's group home has an artificial tree up for the month of December. Certainly, days of trouping out to the woods to cut down an evergreen are just nostalgia for everyone, and it's been years since he's been excited about Christmas. Nevertheless, because I still love the holiday traditions, I had tried to re-create his childhood responses. But he's 50. Do any 50-year-old men get excited about twinkling lights and Christmas ornaments? Christmas dinner definitely and, perhaps, receiving gifts, but Curt gets plenty of that at his home, so he was on his own this year. I called on Christmas day, and he was fine. I'd been up since dawn with my grandchildren across the country. They were really excited about the presents, the tree, the sparkling lights, and smoke puffing from their new model train. They'd dressed the dog in a Santa suit, had eaten several candy canes from their stockings, and were whooping with delight and a sugar surge. It's my time to be a grandmother now, and it's time for Curt to celebrate in his own way, in his own home with his friends. They are paid employees, but most truly care about him and he about them. It is as it should be.

Planning for the End of Your Life

The next chapter in the life of a family is when time reverses the cycle, when children eventually have to take care of parents. I know that time is coming and am trying to prepare for it. I never asked my daughter to take care of her brother or to be his guardian, but when she had a family of her own, she asked to be included as one of his guardians, along with her father and me. Of course, she knows she'll probably outlive her parents and may outlive Curt, but it was her decision. I've made plans to live independently as long as I can and then live in a facility until my death. I know that Curt will be taken care of by the agency that supports him now and that they will make appropriate arrangements for his care because he is officially a ward of the state in which he resides. Laura will have a say in his care but does not have to provide it, physically or financially. Making these plans is not easy, but it's not gruesome or morbid. These plans fit the pattern that started with my parents and feel comfortable and right for me. Do what you deem is right for you and your family, but do something, make a plan, and tell your loved ones so that your dependent child will never be without care.

Curt at 50, outside his home.

Marriage, Partners, Single Parenthood

Note: A disabled child strains marriages and partnerships. Unfortunately, many fathers and some mothers don't make the cut. Today, parenting has come to be more equally shared than it was in the days before the feminist movement. Now, many men are primary parents, but that was unusual when Curt was young. I know very few couples my age who have managed to stay together when dealing with a child with special needs. Looking up statistics is difficult because different research organizations study different populations, and in some cases the stress of a disabled child strengthens a relationship and family. There are many factors that contribute to the dissolution of a marriage or partnership. Therefore, many children with special needs live in single-parent families. Extended families are rare now too; very few children live with both grandparents and parents anymore. Nevertheless, more grandparents by themselves are taking care of their special needs grandchildren than ever before. So single-parent families are compelled to reach out to other groups for support. Organizations of various kinds—educational, religious, neighborhood—can provide support and socialization. Hillary Clinton was right when she said, "It takes a village to raise a child." Read the next chapter.

CHAPTER 4

Others

"Control, Gotta Figure It Out!"

Changing Preconceptions

You may know a lot about child development, medical, political, and educational systems, or you may know as little as I did. I had never even held a child when my son was put into my arms at his birth. I had never been hospitalized or taken care of anyone seriously ill. I was an eighth grade English teacher and had some idea of public school education but not "special education." I was unprepared but not unaware.

When I was in junior high, my Girl Scout troop visited the local state hospital for "retarded" children, a term not acceptable now. A classic Dickensian institution, it was an unforgettable experience that left me with mixed feelings. In a room filled with the noise of children crying and the permeating stench of urine, one little boy captured my heart. He was blond, empty blue eyed, snotty nosed, and wandering around flapping his hands and babbling. I remember saying, "I could never take care of a retarded child!" But 20 years later, it happened, and I knew I couldn't put my child in a place like the one I remembered. In reality, years later, I returned to that same institution, which by then had been down-sized to house only a few residents and the regional dental clinic that serves people with disabilities. The pea-green paint had been painted over, the smell was disinfected, and we had mostly extraordinary dental care from their services.

Slowly and reluctantly, I learned I had to change my preconceptions and figure out how to make educational, political, and medical systems work for my child. If I didn't do it myself, I could rely on someone else to help me; this part took me much longer to understand. You—or someone in your world—will have to learn about your child's diagnosis, either accept it or challenge it, and move forward with the intention of providing the best care you can for your child. Unfortunately, the big picture is that money and politics influence the institutions that provide care. Whether or not you have money, you will need to learn to negotiate necessary educational, medical, and political systems. If you are smart, you will affiliate with other independent organizations that can help you and your family. You need to be knowledgeable, clear, persistent, patient, and flexible.

We live in a world of specialists, enormous amounts of paperwork, and cumbersome systems. In order to get services you and your child will need, unless you can hire an advocate—and they are available—you or someone else you trust will have to navigate these systems. Sometimes, a spouse, parent, friend, or sibling is willing to take this role if you choose not to, but someone has to get the appropriate care needed to keep your child alive and healthy. We have never paid for medical or educational services, although we are a middle-class family. I know of people who have privately paid for all the services for their child, but private pay is not necessarily better than what we have experienced; it too requires vigilance and monitoring.

Our country's government is based on the idea that all citizens have rights and that it is the responsibility of all to contribute financially to provide services. That's not a solely Democratic idea nor is it socialism; it is simply the way the system works/stumbles in this country. It is your responsibility to find care for your child from the many sources that provide it. A hospital social worker can get you started. Your pediatrician's office and school special education department should help when your child is three years old. If your child has a well-known disability, both national and regional chapters will help. In my case, my son's diagnosis was so rare that nobody knew anything about it for years; now there is the Chromosome Disorder Outreach, Inc. organization online, but I still haven't found other people with the exact same diagnosis.

Medical Systems

"Hospital Fears"

Doctors, nurses, medicines, treatments, medical terminology, hospitals, clinics, hours/days of waiting, paperwork, diagnoses, bedpans, ERs, waiting rooms, hospital cafeterias: it's a whole new world with its own vocabulary. It is scary, vitally important, sometimes cold and impersonal, more often intense and overwhelming, and filled with dedicated, overworked people. Welcome to the ever-changing, never-changing world of medical care, the work of life and death. Here are two examples of experiences we had with medical institutions and practitioners: one was positive and one was very frustrating but eventually turned out all right.

Here's the positive story about early childhood and my introduction to the medical system. I don't remember when I wrote it, but it was written as a memory.

> *My son survived his initial "failure to thrive" and is now 6 weeks old, pink and beginning to gain weight. He sputters his lips and gazes at us through thick brown lashes and huge chocolate eyes. We go into Boston to see Dr. F., a genetic specialist who is supposed to confirm the diagnosis of Cornelia de Lange Syndrome that our pediatricians gave us, a projection that our son will be a vegetable and that we should put him away and forget about him. Curt's father and I are very nervous, not looking at one another and only talking about the difficulty of parking on the narrow streets.*
>
> *Dr. F. is short, curly haired and looks directly at me. "How's he doing?" He smiles and starts to examine our scrawny but wiggly son. "Well, it's not Cornelia de Lange," he says immediately. I don't know if I feel relief or what to feel. The doctor and his team examine our 8 lb. son (whom we've already nicknamed "Rascal") part by part, inch by inch. His hairline reaches almost to his eyebrows, and his mutton chops, or sideburns, look odd on a baby. "His father apparently was born the same way, his mother says," I volunteer defensively. Dr. F. continues commenting and questioning, "Not much sucking reflex. Is he taking in food? How are his bowel movements?" They draw blood and fill in the charts. Then Dr. F.*

says, "We will call you to let you know if his blood tests show anything, but I can't give you a diagnosis. You need to love this little guy. Do what you would naturally do. Give him lots of stimulation, and relax. We'll keep track of you and want to see you back here in two months."

The ride home was quiet except for Curt's babbling and sputtering. His Dad and I never were able to talk much about our feelings. Parenting was new territory for both of us. We'd never had to communicate about much except what we wanted for dinner or who to invite over for a cookout and cards next Saturday. We never learned. I did, however, learn to communicate with medical people. Dr. F. guided me to focus on the important issues. Each time we visited for the next twenty-one years, Dr. F. would say, "Hello," look directly at me, and ask, "Is he still learning?" That was the most important question for me.

You will learn to focus on the important questions while keeping track of the many details required in order to respond intelligently and helpfully to the doctors' questions. Of course, things do go wrong, and you will have to reassess and always keep track of all the medical stuff, even if it's from an overview position when your adult child is away from home and under someone else's care.

Here's the negative story from a writing from later on when Curt was in his 40s. He had been living in a group home in the community for many years and was taken to most medical appointments by the caretaking staff. I still try to join them for dental appointments because they are so difficult for Curt and because of this unfortunate incident.

*I am sitting at a medical facility staffed by caring
administrative women, experienced technicians,
institutional furniture, official bulletin boards, a
wall-mounted TV tuned to an educational station,
well-worn magazines, and a multicultural variety
of caregivers attending individuals with disabilities.
The patients are equipped with an intriguing array of
mechanical aids, from electric wheelchairs to Velcro
braces and supports for heads, fingers, arms, etc.
The vulnerable surrounded by metal, technology,
and an amazing collection of individuals assembled
to provide care. It's inspiring, exhausting, expensive,
and I'm always anxious as well as awed. Although I
hate to admit it, I am also proud to be a part of this
system and eager to declare that I am a parent. I am
often delighted to re-meet a nurse or office worker
who remembers my son and our family. We sometimes hug and exchange stories about former doctors,
like, "Remember Dr. Ed? He used to carry Curtis on
his shoulders into the dental chair from the waiting
room!"*

*Today, Curt is going to have a tooth pulled. The deci-
sion to do it was made in January, permission slips
signed and returned by February, first appointment in
March. The day of the first appointment Curt developed bacterial conjunctivitis, and the appointment
was postponed. The second try almost happened, but
the pre-visit medication was mislabeled, reordered,
arrived but with the wrong dosage, and then the staff
member got caught up in traffic. Today is scheduled
appointment #3. I am early and have driven down*

*from New Hampshire. Curt and his caretakers are not
here yet. I'm anxious, not just because I've driven three
hours, but because there is always the possibility that
something could go wrong. Also, I can't imagine how
his caregivers will be able to flush out his mouth once
the extraction actually takes place. I know I really
don't have to worry, that he'll be taken care of, but I
worry anyway.*

*Curtis arrives with staff, and we are escorted into
the dental room. "I'm Dr. X." "Hello Doctor, I'm his
mother, and this is Annette and Victor." "Oh, glad to
meet you. We don't see many parents." Curt is assisted
into a reclined dental chair with the papoose already
in position. Quickly, his hands are Velcroed to his
sides, cloth panels envelop his torso and are Velcroed
tightly. Additionally, a wrap of self-sticking material straps his legs to the chair. Only his head is now
visible above the wrappings. (This is usual procedure;
I'd gone through the legal permission slips to allow
restraints for such procedures because it usually comforts him as well as keeps him from moving.)*

*"It's a wisdom tooth, but it should pop right out,"
the dentist says to the group as he starts to prepare
the Novocain. I cradle Curt's head and say, "The
dentist will numb your mouth with a topical then the
Novocain will hurt for only a moment, so you have
to stay still." "Don't tell him that," the dentist objects.
"You are giving him negative thoughts! Novocain
doesn't hurt." I back away reluctantly, and Annette
and Victor exchange glances.*

Once the Novocain has numbed his mouth, I steady

Curt's head; one staff holds his knees, the other his feet, and the dentist begins to take the offending tooth out. Annette, Victor and I are whispering, "OK, everything's fine. Be still, and it won't take long." "Good job, Big Guy, you're doing fine." "Hold still." Curt screams every time the dentist tries to pull the tooth.

"He's not in pain. It's just pressure," the dentist insists. A crack and a piece of bloodied tooth comes out with the long-handled pliers the dentist is using. He goes back for more. More screams. The tension in the small room builds as the dentist tries harder. The tooth doesn't budge. Finally, without looking up at anyone, the dentist gives up. "We'll have to refer him to an oral surgeon," he says and leaves the room without another word. Annette and I make eye contact in stunned silence, unwrap Curt, and get him back into his wheelchair.

In the lobby, the receptionist gives us a card with an appointment for a consultation with an oral surgeon who takes Medicare. The appointment is in September. It is now early June. "This is not acceptable," I say, but the receptionist says, "It's the best we can do."

Back at his residence, we are shaken but start to get to work to get an oral surgeon to remove the now-broken tooth. Rather quickly, Curt is transferred to dental care at the local hospital where patients with special needs are treated. Apparently, many of the other residents at Curt's house who require sedation for dental appointments are routinely taken as day-stay patients for dental work, so the staff has contacts and Curt gets an appointment. Within weeks, an oral surgeon at the local hospital removes the tooth under general anesthetic. Up until that time he'd had excellent, professional care from the system we were using. He just got a dentist having a bad day.

It was a difficult lesson. I often feel guilty that I didn't stop the dentist earlier when I sensed that all was not going to go well. How many people have to wait from January to September to get a tooth taken care of? I'm afraid many do, many who depend upon government services. The systems are in place and usually provide good care, but we need to be constantly vigilant, patient but persistent. We also need to be forgiving and learn from our mistakes. A few years after the above incident, Curt had another dental crisis, and we had to return to the care of Dr. X. He and I talked briefly about the wisdom tooth incident and agreed to work together to get Curt the best care possible. We all just have to do the best we can.

I constantly struggle with balancing interference and letting go, with being assertive but not aggressive. It's a balance between being proactive and accepting things the way they are. With Curt there are things I can do to relieve his suffering that he can't do himself. Given a choice, Curt would not take any medicine. Without his anticonvulsant medications, we assume he would have multiple seizures, go into status epilepticus—a long seizure a person cannot recover from—perhaps get brain damage and die. We don't know that, of course, but we know that the medications do reduce the intensity and frequency of the seizures. There are side effects to the medication, however, serious ones: his body's vital organs—liver and kidneys, mainly—are being taxed by the constant strain of the medication. It makes Curt slower, may cause headaches and mental confusion. He doesn't need that, but the side effects of having multiple seizures seem to be worse. It's a constant struggle for me. I hate giving him medications; I hate having to remember to do it, to carry the pills, the applesauce, the spoon, and the face wipes. It makes me not want to take any medication myself.

I was responsible for making decisions for him when Curt was younger. However, since he's lived away from home, I've had to switch gears and learn to work with the caregivers who are responsible for him. They have policies and procedures established by their agencies that protect staff and their clients, as well as guidelines set out by federal and state human resources departments. Maintaining clear communication is vital, and I have to change my expectations and give up some of my ways of doing things. In ordinary days or in extraordinary circumstances, it's always a balance.

Educational Systems

In 1975 the federal government passed the EHA (Education for All Handicapped Children Act), which became IDEA (Individuals with Disabilities Educational Act), guaranteeing that every child is entitled to equal opportunities for education from ages three to 22 in the least restrictive setting possible. Appropriate education is personal and is determined by a process called an Individualized Educational Program (IEP) put together by personal in each school setting and worked out with the parent/s. Each state, however, has its own laws about how the federal law is to be interpreted. In Massachusetts the #766 Act is the state version that passed in 1973, the year my son turned three. He was part of the first wave of children who were covered from ages three to 22, and their experiences were entirely different than anyone born before 1970. We were lucky.

The annual IEP is often a high- or low-water marker for families with a child with disabilities. The title is self-explanatory, but each state is different. In Massachusetts an IEP can originate from a parent or a teacher, but the parent/s or legal guardian must sign the bottom line. An IEP is not mandatory, even if there is concern about a child's behavior or progress in school. IEPs are used to provide the "least restrictive environment" for a child's maximum learning. They are also to provide enrichment for gifted students as well as supplemental services for children with different learning styles, developmental delays, and other services. To many people, asking for an IEP and getting a "label" is still a stigma, an indication that something is wrong, and it brings up images of segregation and "special" needs, so some parents do not want to ask for it.

Once in place, the IEP can be modified or changed each year to meet the child's needs. At any point or at any age, a parent can refuse services proposed by the school system. The public school is required to provide an alternative, however. Service requests in an IEP go into a town/city's school budget. They may try to avoid the most expensive options because they have to fit the expense of your child's individualized education into their school budget. There are some federal funds, but much of the special education budget does come from local property taxes. In reality, wealthy school districts can offer more than districts with lower revenues. Parent advisory groups are available for support in some areas. The system is inequitable. You may have to move; families do move to states or towns that provide the best services.

Some parents also refuse to work with the public schools and send their children to private schools serving those with special needs. You may consider the private route, but we decided early on that we didn't want to do that, even though there are many private communities and schools in New England. If you decide not to work with your local school district, you will pay for your child's education and care for his entire lifetime, and most people do not have enough money to adequately do that. And it's not necessary. Our son went to one of the finest, most marvelous residential private schools in New England, and our town paid for it. Taking this route, however, requires a tremendous amount of time, energy, negotiating, pleading, writing letters, marching on the statehouse, etc., as well as establishing a good working relationship with your local special education director. You have to pay attention and advocate constantly. Keeping accurate notes about every meeting or phone call is essential, not a luxury. Of course, you keep the paperwork in one place, make file folders, date all correspondence, organize as best you can, and respond to requests as quickly as you can. It becomes a full-time job on top of your already compelling full-time job of caring for your child.

One of the most wonderful things about this lifelong journey is that your child can also learn to advocate for himself. "But he can't even talk," you say. But he can communicate; he can be a part of the process and, indeed, deserves to be a part of the process. We never know how much another person understands. We can't read another's mind, and we must always treat other people as if they do understand and want to be included in the decisions about their lives. Your child should be informed about this process all along the way. He should go to all his Individualized Educational Program meetings and, later, Individualized Service Program meetings (for ages 23 and older) when he is no longer receiving educational services but still getting "special" services. Your other children and your spouse should be part of this process too so they at least understand what is being asked for and why.

Our local, kind, and efficient special education director and the team that had been responsible for Curt's years of education did an excellent job finding a residential placement for him when I could no longer take care of him at home. Curt had six wonderful years of specialized education and a small, loving, group home before he had to move to another residential setting because he aged out of the educational system.

I always hoped that my husband would do the work of advocacy, but he didn't until we divorced when Curt was 17. At 22 Curt needed to change to a residential program and a day program because the law had determined that he—and all others— had no more need of education at that age. At that time Curt's father did a great job and found a loving home and stimulating day program for Curt near where he grew up and where he still lives today.

The system does work. You have to stay vigilant, contribute, and support the services that are available. That means volunteering, communicating, serving on the board of directors of local human service agencies, marching on the statehouse, etc. The bottom line is that it takes more than a family to care for some people, and that's not a judgment of the family but a tribute to the many caring people in our democratic society who care about others who need their help.

Politics and Allocation of Public Funds

Myth: There is nothing one person can do to help eliminate the barriers confronting people with disabilities.

Fact: Everyone can contribute to change. You can help remove barriers by:

- **Understanding the need for accessible parking and leaving it for those who need it**
- **Encouraging participation of people with disabilities in community activities by using accessible meeting and event sites**
- **Understanding children's curiosity about disabilities and people who have them**
- **Advocating a barrier-free environment**
- **Speaking up when negative words or phrases are used about disability**
- **Writing producers and editors a note of support when they portray someone with a disability as a "regular person" in the media**
- **Accepting people with disabilities as individuals capable of the same needs and feelings as yourself and hiring qualified disabled persons whenever possible**

~Easterseals.com

If you haven't thought of it by now, you won't want to hear this, but you or someone in your support network will have to get involved with the part of our political system that provides human services funds. Some mothers of disabled children become professional advocates, politicians, or educational specialists. For three years I worked in a state-sponsored preschool that integrated severely physically disabled children and regular children. It was a truly amazing place that both my children adored. Curt's sister was there with us, and she learned to read at age four. It was an intense, lively place that encouraged all the children to take risks, be empathetic, and have fun. The preschool was supported by the human service's budget and we continually had to fight for state funding.

Here's a story about advocacy written in the 1970s, about the time Curt was four or five years old:

Curt was small for his age but dead weight; he didn't hold on when in my arms. It was like carrying a large rag doll filled with wet cement, but that rag doll laughed and made chuckling noises, drooled, cooed, "Ma-mah," and took in the world with much laughter and a love of life. He didn't walk until he was six years old, so this Boston trip was certainly when he was younger than that. By that time we had an umbrella stroller, but the steps leading up the state capitol were wide, and there must have been a hundred of them. On this adventure we were ascending the steps to see our state representative to protest potential cuts to spending for the department of human services budget. Actually, most years were touch and go; last minute votes determined whether our small day program for children with severe physical disabilities would continue. We were one of five preschools in the

state that included "temporarily able-bodied" children
with disabled children. Our representative was "on the
fence" about funding this experimental program, so
we'd organized to visit the statehouse on this date.
It took a while to get up the stone steps. Sometimes, I
pushed; other times, I pulled. We reached the heavy
doors, and a kind soul helped me through. We found
the elevator and our representatives' office in Room
531, far away from the entry. When the secretary led
us into the office, our representative barely looked
up from his cluttered desk as I spoke about the
program. Suddenly, the door opened and the sec-
retary announced that the press was here because
there were other "protestors" like me in the building.
Immediately, my representative stood up, smiled, took
my hand, and picked up Curtis for a photo opportu-
nity. We got our funding—and I hope Curt drooled on
his suit.

My friends from the preschool and I did a lot of politicking
in those years, but it was two hours of commuting in a VW bus
with poor heat, so it was difficult. But the effort was worth it
because It certainly helps to get to know your state senators
and representatives. Now, electronic communication with
senators and representatives is easy, but there is nothing like
introducing your child in person to the people who control
the funds for providing his education and health care. You
can't expect others to do it for you, but you don't have to let it
dominate your life. Remember that balance is critical, but there
probably will be times when you really need to put activism on
your Must Do List. Easterseals has regional offices and offers
many services as well as advocacy.

NOTE: The major difference between medical and educational services is that most medical decisions have to be made rather quickly, and educational decisions take lots of time and planning. In the world of special education, the onus of responsibility is on the parent, and services cannot be provided without the parent's approval, but you usually have time to prepare and research. In contrast, once one is admitted to a hospital, protocols are in place, so the choices are fewer. Unfortunately, I've found that even with all the electronic recordkeeping of the day, medical facilities frequently don't have accurate information about medications, past surgeries, procedures, allergies, and undated tests. Calling ahead to make sure test results are in the office before you see the specialist—or taking copies with you—is worth the time it takes. Being knowledgeable and using appropriate terminology in both the medical and political systems adds to your effectiveness and credibility. Keeping good records and being able to give the professionals facts certainly helps.

Other Organizations and the Outside World

"Curt at Special Olympics"

Last but not least in this chapter are the many organizations that can support you, your child, and your family. When Curt was little, I don't remember much that anyone said to me in the way of advice, except that my dad said, "Join a church. You'll need it." It didn't take long to appreciate what he said. My church quickly became a strong support for me spiritually and also provided me with friends, babysitters, and a social outlet for our whole family. There were times when it meant simply an hour of free babysitting, but they were precious hours. Fifty years later, my church still provides much appreciated comfort and support and helps me keep life's ups and downs in perspective.

Many organizations can contribute to the enjoyment and general well-being of your family. Other than the church, when Curt was growing up, I can't remember any organizations that helped me after the wonderful preschool that was sponsored by our state's department of public health. I didn't know of other support organizations except Special Olympics, which provided memorable moments for us. I spent as much time as I could involved in my artistic interests, and those related organizations supported me greatly. Now, there are many groups to support children with specific disabilities such as single parent clubs, education-related parent groups, and religious, fraternal, and political organizations where like-minded people can gain from one another's experiences. If you don't find a group that fits your needs, start one. There are groups that will help financially. The internet is a wealth of information and referrals, but person-to-person support can make your life easier. Isolation doesn't help you, your child, or your family. The greater "village" is out there, but you have to open your door and your heart to let it in.

A fortunate result of unfortunate circumstances is the increased awareness and availability of organizations that support the inclusion of disabled people in sports activities.

Back in 1977, the son of a friend of mine and his father started racing competitively together. They formed Team Hoyt; Dick, the father, would push his son Rick, who had cerebral palsy, in a specialized stroller and run races. Since then, they have gone on to compete in 257 triathlons. Back in the '70s, they were an unusual phenomenon. In Wikipedia, Dick announced that the Boston marathon in 2014 was going to be their last, but they went on to compete, and 2019 was the first Boston Marathon that Rick has missed; he had pneumonia. I do think it's a bit too bad that people recognize Rick Hoyt's name because of his racing with his father but not that he graduated from Boston University. But that's probably because I have never been a runner.

Today, there are many more men and women with disabilities in sports. Many participants are amputees from various wars and accidents, but athletes with developmental disabilities are also included in many of these organizations. There is a branch of NEHSA (New England Healing Sports Association) where I live that enables individuals with disabilities to participate in all snow sports, plus canoeing and kayaking in summer. I'm looking forward to being able to take Curt someday because he loves to move fast or be in water. Nationally, Disabled Sports USA and Adaptive Sports USA have now merged to become Move United.

There are countless organizations available online that provide information about various aspects of care and specific medical help. Be sure to always check on the source, however. Anyone can post a site and cite statistics, but you don't necessarily want to believe information just from an individual (like me!) Care.com gives a description of ten resources that are helpful for parents. Each diagnosis has its own national organization and may have local support.

Curt's chromosome abnormality is so rare that it wasn't until November of 2016 that we got another study and an official diagnosis:

35.8 MB interstitial deletion on the long arm of #13 arr[hg19]13q13.3q21.33 (33, 977, 208-71, 784,165)X1.

If anyone reading this has a link to another individual with this diagnosis, please let me know, or let me know how I can get this information to researchers who will add it to the database of abnormalities. I am looking forward to contacting UNIQUE—Rare Chromosome Disability Support Group in England (www.rarechromo.org) and Chromosome Disorder Outreach, Inc. (www.chromosomedisorder.org) My next task is getting specific medical and developmental information about Curt's 50 years to an appropriate database.

Just this year, Curt's father found information that may put Curt into a very large collection of people united by the same experience, an organization of sorts. In the mid-1970s after the Viet Nam War, information about Agent Orange's effects on humans became more available. Curt's father wondered if his exposure could have indirectly caused Curt's rare chromosome abnormality, because Curt was conceived right after his father returned from Viet Nam. He could not get any answers from the Navy at that time. Now, 50 years later, there is litigation to try to get compensation for victims of that lethal chemical. This important development may finally give us an explanation, but it doesn't change much for me except to give me appreciation for the possibilities of data collection in an increasingly electronically connected world. It's a world of great potential for change and real connections that you can explore for support.

The world has a fast-growing problematic disability, which forges bonds in families, causes people to communicate in direct and clear ways, cuts down meaningless social interactions, pushes people to the limit with learning about themselves, whilst making them work together to make a better world. It's called Autism—and I can't see anything wrong with it, can you? Boy I'm glad I also have this disability!

~Patrick Jasper Lee

The quote above is from a young man with autism. His opinion of a disability that would improve the world—and its organizations—is a world that communicates simply and directly and includes all people; it is a worldview that I support. It could be a blueprint for many organizations in a model world. Currently in our country, there are many who do not support inclusion of any kind; there are millions who want to stay in groups who look and act alike and believe the same things. The list of what they do not want included in their world includes anyone who is different. It is not a principle that formed our country. In spite of progress to integrate disabled individuals into society, I fear that the task may become even more difficult. You are an ambassador; your child is a teacher. Take every opportunity you get to engage in organizations that uphold your values and the dignity of all human life.

CHAPTER 5

Practical Matters

If you are reading this, you probably want to *do something*, right? In spite of the previously mentioned reference to "cleaning out the attic peacefully," my guess is that many readers will skip to this section just to get some help and do something. Perhaps you are thinking, "Anything will help!" Remember that this is advice from someone else who has gone through it, but it may not suit your temperament or circumstances.

We are all very distinctive when it comes to practical coping skills. I have done reasonably well in emergency situations; I'm calm and efficient in a crisis. Unfortunately, I am lousy at regular routines and repetitive chores. I have always resisted the concept of ordinariness and used to equate it with boredom. It took a long time for me to understand the value of coping with and appreciating little things. Please keep that in mind and realize that not only will your child have his own personality, strengths, and weaknesses, but also that you are a unique individual with your own preferences and vulnerabilities that affect how you function with practical matters.

Keeping your child alive is instinctively the most important job you have, but keeping your child happy and alert comes in as a close second. Quality of life is a phrase tossed about in all human services for a reason. The quality of your child's life is linked with you, your family or support people, your neighborhood, school system, and community. In this chapter, experiences about practical matters might help you balance and manage your child's needs. I was a slow learner about taking practical steps to make family life easier and asking for help. Please try to hear this: *you don't have to do it all yourself*. Somebody else can carry out these suggestions and provide help; you do not have to do it all alone.

Develop a Communication System

Not being able to talk sucks. There's no doubt about that. There's a lot of times when I almost feel like I'm trapped inside of myself. Like if I don't talk or yell or scream or laugh, I'm going to explode. A lot of the time it almost feels like I'm suffocating.

~Keary Taylor, *What I Didn't Say*

It may seem ludicrous that I'm starting out with communication. After all, my son was diagnosed to be a vegetable, and who needs to communicate with a vegetable? Firstly, no person is a vegetable. No matter how disabled your child is, speak to him as you would another person. Certainly, some people need one-, two-, or three-step directions at times; but the more naturally you can communicate, the easier it will be for you. That being said, as you would with any person, teach him to communicate his needs, and teach him to identify his world. Curt made lots of noise from day one—babbling, sputtering, yowling, playing with his lips—but at his very best he could only speak less than 50 words. "Dad-dah" is still his best word. Finding some means of communication is one of the best things you can do for your child, yourself, and your family.

When Curt was young there was still a debate about whether or not sign language was helpful for the hearing impaired. There was little consideration of using it for any population other than those with hearing impairments. Now, many pediatricians encourage all moms to teach their babies simple sign language. Do it. Use your hands as well as your voice. Show your child how to make the sign with his tiny hands. Why not? A baby's sensory system is just learning to interact with the world. I have many lists from years of trying to communicate, but always on the list are the words eat, drink, toilet, bed, and seizure. Happy is also a good one. Book, music, or play comes next. Curt's favorite sign/word/place-to-be is car. Other favorites were turtle and elephant— not necessary for daily life but fun to say and sign. Give your child as much help developing a way to communicate as you can: communication boards—either electronic or plain old paper boards—with pictures are good alternatives and complements to signing, as are computers. New technology can be an amazing help as well.

We learned sign language as a family when Curt was about five years old. It was clear that his expressive ability did not match his receptive knowledge—which means he understood more than he could communicate. Shortly after we'd been using basic sign language, Curt was hospitalized again, this time to remove his adenoids in hopes of decreasing his frequent earaches. In the hospital he refused to eat or drink after surgery because his throat hurt. The nurses kept offering Jell-O, something he never ate at home with my improved nutrition knowledge. I remember seeing him standing in a crib in his hospital gown, holding onto the railing—he was small and still could not walk by himself. He looked up at me and signed, "Cereal." Against the wishes of the nurses, I got him cereal and milk, which he ate. He was soon back to normal again.

I have known many individuals with no verbal skills and extremely limited physical control of their limbs, but communication is so important that any system is better than none. In my art therapy practice, most of my clients had their own "visual language" of shapes and colors that enabled them to "say" what they needed to say to be heard when they were painting. Your child's "art" is a form of communication, too. Just say, "Tell me about that?" rather than, "Is that a kitty cat?" What you thought was a cat may be his little sister. One of my granddaughter's favorite books is *Out of My Mind* (2012) by Sharon M. Draper. It's about a fifth-grade girl who has cerebral palsy and is unable to move much of her body independently and is unable to talk. The story is written for teenage readers and deals with the frustrations of this young woman as she struggles to go to school and be her fullest self. She is not just intelligent; she is very, very intelligent. When given the choice of getting technical aid for either walking or talking, she immediately chooses talking, and her life changes.

If you are reading this and are concerned about someone with recent onset communication issues—intellectual disabilities, stroke recovery, Alzheimer's, etc.— certainly consider signing or some form of communication board for communication, plus any help you can get from electronic media. Simple sign language, computers, communication boards, books—anything to match a sound/movement/blink to meaning. There are educational specialists to help, so take advantage of everything. Make up your own system, ask your other kids, observe, and develop a communication system to give anyone you care about the ability to tell you and others what he needs. I always dream of Curt miraculously being able to talk clearly, but I imagine that if he did, the first thing he'd say would be, "Mom! Do *not* point out every cow that goes by the car window. I don't care about cows anymore. I'm not a child!"

[Here is writing from a time when Curt was 45 (11/1/16)]

*"Are you finished?" I ask, although the answer is
obvious. We are at Boston Market. Both Curt and I
have eaten every salty, mushy morsel of our dinners
of mashed garlic potatoes, creamed spinach, and
meatloaf softened up with gravy. Only a few crumbs
of cornbread are scattered on the floor. I pull his chair
away from the table and wipe his chin with the napkin
soaked with drool that I had anchored under his chin.
Getting him on his feet, we head for the door. I'm
feeling happy and encouraged that he is able to walk
again, because the last time we were here, Curt was in
a wheelchair. My optimism is flagging because each
step is so arduous. I stand in front of him, holding both
hands, and propel him forward slowly. The restaurant
manager, Holly, comes over to hold open the heavy
glass doors. Curt smiles at her, giggles, and grabs her
hand, so the three of us stagger through the door into
the chill of October's night.*

*Finally to the car, Curt refuses to get in. I'm embar-
rassed and completely unable to get him to move.
He outweighs me and is very strong. I look at Holly
helplessly. She doesn't know how to respond. Curt is
backing up towards the restaurant when I think to
say, "Curtis, what do you want? What's the matter?"
He looks directly at me, releases a hand, and signs,
"Toilet." With relative ease we retrace our steps, he
uses the toilet, we say goodbye and thanks to Holly
again, and get into the car. "It never hurts to ask," I
say to myself as I apologize to him and relax.*

Another powerful way to get your child to learn about the world and communicate is to read to him every day. Read frequently and with variety and interest in your voice. From the earliest simple picture books to children's stories, magazines, picture dictionaries, any librarian can help you with age-appropriate books. Remember though that your child at 18 may be developmentally more like a 10-year-old; my opinion is that the message of the story is more important than the age appropriateness. As you read, say, "Where is the bear?" or "What sound does a bear make?" Even if you get no response, something is enriching your child's brain. There is a powerful distinction between reading to a person and watching TV or a video together; reading is more stimulating, even if the individual you are reading to seems not to understand every word.

Footnote: Don't talk baby talk to anyone to anyone, regardless of their age or how infantile they may be acting.

Learn about Talking to Others

Myth: Curious children should never ask people about their disabilities.

Fact: Many children have a natural, uninhibited curiosity and may ask questions that some adults consider embarrassing. But scolding curious children may make them think having a disability is "wrong" or "bad." Most people with disabilities won't mind answering a child's question.

~Easterseals.com

I'm afraid it is true that you will get a lot of stares if your child's disability shows physically or if your child acts in an unusual manner. The general public doesn't know what to do or say about a person who looks or acts different in any way. I'm convinced that all wars and divisiveness in our crazy world would be eliminated if we could just understand that differences are a part of being alive. Tulips don't hate crocuses or the rabbits that nibble their heads off, but they can't talk and we can. When someone looks with disgust or curiosity at your child or asks, "What's wrong with him?" you can respond. I've often wished that I had a remark that would suddenly lift the clouds of ignorance and bring in universal love and understanding, but I usually say something simple like, "Curt has a disability, so his muscles don't work well together. He is smart and funny, though." Please don't get onto a lecture box and think you have to tell everybody everything. A few times when Curt was a child, other kids didn't notice his differences. One time at the beach, a little kid joined us where we were making sand castles. He played for a while then looked up, and I thought he was going to ask me about Curt's disabilities. I had a prepared explanation but didn't expect, "What's wrong with his little toe?" That one was easy! The best teachers learn to answer the questions their students ask before trying to teach anything else.

Many times, people don't ask but avoid eye contact and move away. Don't let that distress you; you don't need that kind of negative energy. More and more often lately, I meet someone's eyes and smile. A surprising number of strangers say, "I have a son with cerebral palsy," or "My cousin uses a wheelchair too." I missed many chances for education when I was younger and either self-conscious about my son or trying to enlighten everyone about the world of the differently abled, but I eventually learned how to respond better, whether it was a negative or positive comment. More and more people understand, but we need to keep educating the ignorant.

You can also educate and enlighten on a one-to-one basis, as illustrated in the following memory: Curt and his sister were probably one and three years old, so I put them both in a baby carriage, facing one another. At that time they didn't have harnesses or seatbelts, but they sat there happily.

I remember a shopping trip in a crowded store where the aisles were narrow and cash registers piled high with impulse purchase displays. A young cashier was checking me out in more ways than one. Perhaps we all do that, look at a person and make assumptions? She was all smiles and chattering nonsense as she rang up the merchandise I'd pushed onto the conveyer belt. I pushed the carriage ahead to be able to pay and pick up my merchandise. When she could see the two kids in the carriage, she literally paled and started to tear up as she stared at Curt. "I had no idea. I didn't know. I'm sorry," she stammered. "I just thought you had it all. You looked like you were one of the lucky ones. I just assumed, I'm so sorry," she blubbered on. Without hesitation, I reached out to touch her arm and said, "I *am* one of the lucky ones. You were right," paid for my purchases, and pushed the carriage out of the store.

Don't wait for people to be friendly, show them how.

~Henry James

That was a good experience that certainly counter-balanced the many times when Curt's presence in a store or restaurant caused patrons to look away, turn away, or move to the other side of the store. I have never had anyone verbally or physically abuse Curt, although I know that abuse happens and seems to be happening more and more as our country goes through a wave of hatred of anyone who looks or acts different from the norm. In many ways we have come a long way in the years since Curt was born. Now that there are laws mandating that all children with disabilities have a right to the least-restrictive education, more and more disabled children are mainstreamed into regular school classrooms. Laws about access to public places have enabled physical access to thousands, but it takes time for change. Our job is to continue to educate and advocate for inclusion.

In another way we—and Curt—are lucky. His disabilities are seen ones. There are many disabilities that are not visible, such as mental illness, autism, and learning disabilities. These disabilities can cause severe or mild patterns of behavior or cognitive impairment, but the person "looks normal." The unseen disabilities are even harder to understand and include in daily life, but part of our job as parents is educating others about inclusion of all people.

Balancing Stimulating and Soothing

You may soon learn what upsets, stimulates, or soothes your child—and you. Music, color, good smells, gentle or firm touch, tasty food, and everything that stimulates the senses make a contribution to a person's well-being. Music has always been Curt's favorite stimulation, except for being with loved ones. He was slow to sit, crawl, and cruise, and did not walk until he was six years old. Before that, we tried everything from putting toys just out of reach to patterning—repetitive patterns to develop neurological responses—but his legs were not strong enough, his feet were misshapen, and his balance was inadequate. He got those ugly metal braces and brown leather shoes that must have been worn by Tiny Tim back in Dickens' day, and they helped.

One of the things we tried to get him to support his weight and strengthen his legs was an apparatus called a Jolly Jumper. It is a harness around the trunk that supports the body upright with feet just touching the floor. The harness is attached to a bar suspended from the ceiling with a spring. The idea is that the child will kick or push against the floor, bounce up and down again to stimulate the legs into a pattern that would encourage walking. Curt just hung there, babbling away, day after day, for what seemed like months. (Of course, I didn't put him in it for very long at a time.) During the day, I routinely listened to public radio tuned to the classical station that I loved. Curt seemed to like the music, and I assumed he found it soothing. One spring day when Curt was in the Jolly Jumper, I flipped the radio to a pop station, and *Jeremiah Was a Bullfrog* by Three Dog Night was playing. Curt's head turned toward the music, and he giggled. He must have just kicked spontaneously, and the Jolly Jumper bounced up. He kicked again, and again. He started jumping then and hasn't stopped. Even now, when he has trouble walking, when he's happy, he jumps with delight. Note to self: change the channel every now and then.

Another obvious stimulation is the toys that your child has to play with. Try different, colorful, interesting things. Rig up toys so that they can be seen and touched. Make mobiles for overhead out of household objects or sparkly things, put pictures on the wall, use printed bedsheets, and try items that smell, sound, and feel stimulating or soothing. Perhaps your child will find a favorite toy or blanket, but try to introduce him to new things and experiences. If he's sitting in a highchair while you cook, show him the veggies, let him smell, touch, taste, and see them. Talk to him as you cook, do laundry, wash dishes, and of course let him play in the water and learn to love his bath. Remember to play even traditional games and involve him with other children and siblings.

Laura and Curt played Hide-and-Seek for years. Laura was almost two years younger but more able and smarter; nevertheless, it took her a while before she figured out that when it was his turn to "seek," Curt would dramatically slap his hands over his eyes and peek through his fingers to see where she was hiding. He was always able to find her.

If money is a problem in providing toys, be creative or ask for help. Civic organizations, churches, or neighbors might get him a tricycle, swing set, or computer. Other people can help you and might find it easiest to help with providing *things* when they don't know how else to help.

Remember that your child's experience with the environment will be different from yours, but be prepared to learn for yourself. Try to understand your child's sensory issues and imagine what it is like to be in his place.

"Caterpillar Playing Hide and Seek"

[Written on 5/11/15, about a toy the kids had when they were much younger]

The gizmo was bright yellow, red, green, and blue plastic, Lego colors, like most toddler toys. Advertised as educational, the toy had five snap-up Jack-in-the-Box style compartments that would open if the child performed the correct small-motor task. It was well designed, annoying, and durable. Curt loved that toy for years, really years. One compartment opened with a lever and a clown popped out with a squeak. The American Sign Language sign for "clown" is honking one's nose, so Curt slapped his nose every time the clown appeared. Under the cover opened by the push button was a zebra; the up-down gizmo made a buzz for the lion that appeared. "Lion" was one of Curt's better words, and he would say it faithfully. I can't remember the other compartments, except one had a telephone dial, a skill no longer valuable. For the years that he played with that thing, he never learned to close the individual doors after he'd opened them. Guess who did that? Every time I saw the toy with doors open, I'd snap them shut. Sometime later, I'd hear a familiar thwack and excited holler, and know that Curt had rediscovered a favorite lion or zebra hidden in the toy. He eventually grew tired of it and moved on to another toy, but now I look back and wonder if he was just playing a game with me for all those years.

Stimulating and soothing activities should always be balanced, but when you are exhausted, it is easiest to go for the activities that calm. Remember that exercise for everyone and just being outside is often a good choice—and free. This is a delicate balance of energies, and it is constantly changing. Pay attention, be creative, and try not to be discouraged.

Milestones: Are they important?

What would happen, they conjectured, if they simply went on assuming their children would do everything. Perhaps not quickly, perhaps not by the book. But what if they simply erased those growth and developmental charts, with their precise, constricting points and curves? What if they kept their expectations but erased the time line? What harm could it do? Why not try?

~Kim Edwards, *The Memory Keeper's Daughter*

I was lucky in a way. I knew almost nothing about child development. Curt was my first child; my parents helped but never interfered. His disability was so rare that there was never any idea of what to anticipate about his life expectancy, much less his development, so I just hoped for the best and tried to keep him learning and growing at his own pace. Certainly, learn about child development and help your child move to the next skill level if possible, but don't get distressed or discouraged. Your child may plateau for periods of time or even regress. It is helpful if you can document development. (See next section.) Get help from the many experts available in medical and educational settings. (See Chapter 4. OTHERS.) But try not to get stressed out about so-called milestones or let comparisons take you away from the day-to-day joys.

[From 10/17/12]

Curtis took his first independent steps on June 6, 1976. He was almost six years old. He'd been hospitalized again for dehydration and drug toxicity and returned home after 10 days with less seizure medication and more energy. He and his younger sister, Laura, attended East Mountain Preschool ... and I worked there in the Resource Room for Parents.
For some reason, that day Delia, a staff member, brought Curt into the Resource Room where I worked. They were at the door, and I on the other side of the room. Delia held Curt's hands, guiding him to walk, and said quietly, "OK, Curtis, walk to Mommy." She let go of his hands, and he quickly walked unaided across the room to my hands. There was utter silence in the room. Tears were steaming down my face and Delia's, but I turned Curtis around and said quietly, "Now walk back to Delia." He got halfway back across the room before he fell over. Delia and I screamed, hollered, cried, and smothered him with kisses. It was quite a moment.

After that day, he almost ran everywhere ... arms out, hands flapping, grinning widely and legs flying in his institutional brown leather boots attached to the metal braces up to his knees. We have lots of pictures from that joyous time. We waited a long time for that milestone.

Perhaps we should change the term "Milestones" to "Changes"? Curt's milestones were far from the norm, but he kept advancing until he was in his 40s, when his physical stresses—and a bad medication—caused him to start losing skills. Since then, he has lost skills and his physical and communication abilities have diminished. It's been difficult to observe, and I imagine it must be difficult for him, although he seems to be happy. The staff usually chuckles and says, "He's just slowing down," which is understandable.

I found the following comments when I was cruising the internet for supportive quotes. The quote below made me uncomfortable because I have always been pushing Curt to be active and have not wanted him to be dependent upon a walker or wheelchair. This quote reminded me that my goals might not be appropriate or helpful for my son:

"First Month Walking, Six Years Old"

My mother was determined that I should be able to walk two miles. If you could walk two miles, she said, you could get to most places you needed to get to. Actually, this is a fallacy. The fact that you can, with great difficulty, and taking an unconscionably long time about it, walk two miles will not get you anywhere you need or, at any rate, want to go. There were times when a wheelchair would have added another dimension to my life, but that was a forbidden subject; and it was not until many, many years later, long after my father and I were alone, that I took the law into my own hands and bought one; and instantly, dazzled with the new freedom that it brought me, swept my father off to his old haunts on an Hellenic cruise.

~Rosemary Sutcliff, *Blue Remembered Hills: A Recollection*

I fought for years to keep Curt eating regular food and walking independently, but I had to abandon both those goals because of his body's needs and the safety of those who take care of him.

I really push him to keep moving and to stay as independent as possible, but he's learned how to enjoy group-home living and how to let others help him. He now uses a wheelchair and eats only pureed foods. I had to re-assess my goals for him with the help of other caregivers. We both have aged, and the stresses on the body are taking their toll. Be cautious about milestones or other comparative measures; remember that they are statistics based on averages. Use the physical aids available to make everything easier and live with what *is*.

Details, Record Keeping and the Big Picture

It's hard to keep records, but it's vitally important for your own information and your doctors and teachers. Your records have to be as accurate and helpful as possible. They don't need to be lengthy, but it's difficult to separate medical from emotional, the details from the bigger picture.

How can you be aware without being overly cautious and always worrying? Small details add up, so keeping good records is essential. It's impossible to answer a doctor's question, "Was he better on the dose of five mgs or ten mgs?" without accurate records. For example, a simple calendar with checks for seizures and the date and dosage will tell you if the seizures increased or decreased with a medication change. It is a nuisance, of course, keeping all those records, but it's critical. Doctors have tests, physical examinations, and their experience to help them; but as the parent, you are the most help. "He had more seizures" is not as helpful as "He had thirty-two seizures last week, half of them were just as he woke up in the morning, and the rest were late in the afternoon." Patterns make a difference, especially in the administration of medicines.

"Is he more alert?" is also a difficult question to answer without some specific measures. To me, most important of all is what I call a QOL index, a Quality of Life Index—I think I made that up. It can be as simple as a Bad Day, an OK Day, or a Great Day (1, 2 or 3) on that same calendar. In most situations, that's all you need. Maybe breaking it down into morning, midday, and night would help, but KISS: Keep It Simple, Sister. If your child is in school, you will need to develop a simple system so you know what happened when he was not at home. The school may have a system for keeping track of seizures or other medical/reportable incidents, but a notebook with either a check list or a few comments helps you know if you child had a good day, an OK day, or a very bad, horrible day. Make up your own system. For years I noted on the seizure calendar when thunderstorms were present and, eventually, was able to show the doctors that Curt's seizures increased just before a thunderstorm (barometric pressure).

Learn how medicines affect the body, read about how long a medication takes to be effective, notice drug interactions. Your neurologist may not notice that your child takes Benadryl for allergies and that might affect the anticonvulsant he is prescribing. Keep your facts as straight as you can, but remember the QOL. I have almost always wanted my son to be alert, active, and happy more than I want him to be seizure free. You'll have to make that decision for yourself, but at least think about priorities.

Safety and Risk Taking

Is keeping him safe more important than keeping him happy? In theory it's not much different from allowing a normal child to get dirty playing in the mud or falling off a bicycle while learning to ride. As a matter of fact, is there a reason why your child with developmental disabilities can't play in the mud or learn to ride a bike? Sometimes, there is; sometimes, there is not. Consider adaptions but take some risks. Curt still puts things in his mouth but has never swallowed anything. He's not stupid and has turned out to be amazingly resilient. Your child certainly needs reasonable safeguards, but balance that care with interaction with the world.

Friends always tell me that if I ever write my own autobiography, it would be titled, *She Always Took the Stairs.* Even if there is an elevator, I usually climb the stairs, even when I'm tired, because it's good exercise. That's just plain silly. Don't be as stubborn as I am about doing things and getting equipment that will make life easier for everyone in the family:

[Written on 4/11/2015 about Curt's earlier childhood]

We lived [from the time Curt was 4 until he was 31] in an old, drafty house looking out over the whole Connecticut River Valley. On a clear day we could see the Berkshires; on many a windy night, we felt the westerly winds coming from the mountains and smacking into the backside of the house. We were perched on the edge of the ridge and our land dropped off precipitously on the far side ... but there was what we called a back yard. It was a great back yard to play in, even though only a small part of it was what a city person would call grass. Most of it was mowed field with lots of rocks pushing up through the dirt.

Because of the rocks, field grass, and hills, neither child ever had much of a chance to ride a bike. Curt had a red plastic Sit'n'Spin; he could sit in it, turn the wheel with his good left arm, and go around and around in circles on the open cement porch. They both had other plastic low-to-the-ground vehicles to go up past the sandbox on the high side of the hill and careen down to the other side past the maple tree. Laura managed to avoid the tree; Curt hit it over and over again. He would crash, fall off the Big Wheel, laugh, and say, "More!" He couldn't walk until he was 6 years old, but he loved to ride that vehicle long before he could walk, and I carried both him and the Big Wheel back up to the top of the hill over and over again.

Sometimes, we would play baseball as a family. We would put something down near the porch steps as

Home Plate. First base was the maple tree, second base was a flat rock ... and third base was a rock poking out near the sandbox. We had a whiffle ball and fat bat.

Their dad built a sandbox into the side of the hill next to a large rock; it had side seats and lasted for years. Both kids dug and filled and dumped with delight. Curt liked to help me with my perennial border gardens. Cosmos, dianthus, peonies, lupines, iris, chrysanthemums, sedums, and daisies somehow survived erratic watering, poor soil, and wind. Around the ugly cement porch, I grew enormous, dinner-plate dahlias and tried to grow peas. Often Curt and I sat side by side and pulled weeds. I had to always be out there with the kids so they wouldn't wander off, which gave me plenty of time to garden.

One day in August, after the paternal grandparents visited on their annual trip ... I picked up our local weekly paper and read, "Free to a Good Home: Shepherd Collie found abandoned at Mall." ... We didn't need a dog, but we got the dog. Laura named her "Tiffany," and she was a beauty! Collie-expressive eyes, soft floppy ears, thin face, a little shepherd bulk and a long wispy tail with white, plume-like "feathers" that matched the "feathers" on her legs. She was big, gentle, already trained, and an emotional support for me more than anything else.

It soon became apparent that collies run and that we needed some way to contain the dog. I had resisted paying for a fence for years because it was ridiculously expensive. My mom helped us pay for a fence to *contain the dog. What a difference that fence made in my life! I could put both kids outside, usually see them from the kitchen window and relax, knowing they were probably safe even when I couldn't see them. Laura could open the door to get back inside or call me if she needed anything. Curt was so happy to be able to go where he wanted without me tagging along. A good deal of the time he picked up sticks and wacked them against the side of the maple tree. Laura spent hours on the tire swing. The dog played with both of them. Soon after, we got two sister cats, so there was a lot of activity in that backyard. And the dog? She could easily jump the fence, but she never did.*

Years after the decision to fence in the back yard, the simple ordinary pleasures of family life with time to play outside, play ball, swing, and nuzzle with a dog gave us all delight. Both kids learned how to entertain themselves as well as how to play together as a family.

"Curt and Tiffany"

Vacations and Fun

Please don't let the special needs of one person in your family override opportunities to do stuff together as a family and to have some fun or get away. It's equally important to take some time to get away just with your spouse (or friends) and away from the children. If you can't include the disabled family member, get someone to care for him while the rest of you get away. Be creative.

Try to do as much as you can together as a family. Having other families as friends is wonderful and provides delightful times of shared meals, games, and friendship. It also spreads out the responsibilities for special care and gives you other eyes to help with a child who needs constant supervision. Nevertheless, going on a vacation is exciting for everyone and the stuff of family memories and stories. A "staycation," a vacation within driving distance but not overnight, can also work. The internet has loads of sites with low-cost ideas for staycations at home. Use these ideas for school holidays and snow days. You don't have to be wealthy to have a rich family life. Plan for fun, take time for vacations.

Every year from the time Curt was born, we spent our summer vacation week camping in Maine. Curt's father's parents were there for their summer vacation, so we would get a chance to see them as well as be in one of our most favorite places. And camping was cheap back then.

One year we had to take two cars for some reason. The plan was good, if not well thought out. All the camping gear, clothes for beach days and chilly nights, sand toys and books for the two children, food for the week, and of course, Curt's medications for his seizure disorder were piled into the two cars. I had Curt with me, and Curt's sister and her father were in the second car. We left at the same time, but it's difficult to try to travel in tandem, and it was before cell phones, so once we left, we had no communication. Traffic got between us, and I lost track of the other car but trusted that we'd both get there about the same time. The drive was over three hours. When Curt and I got to our regular campground, the owners greeted us with their usual friendliness and a telephoned message from Curt's father: "Car broke down. We'll be there tomorrow." I assessed what was actually in my car. I had Curt, his medicine—the only critically important item—some food, one double sleeping bag and an air mattress, but no tent, cooking gear, or flashlights.

The campground owners were sympathetic and generous. They said that for one night we could use a tent they had already set up at one of the campsites in the open field. We gratefully accepted the shelter and went out to eat then back to get settled in before dark. Curt just loved camping and being outside and was unperturbed about our change of plans and accommodations. I got the air mattress blown up with much huffing and puffing and his laughter. We settled into the double sleeping bag just as darkness fell. The night was cool and damp; we thought we could hear the ocean's waves and smell the salt air. We were tired and fell asleep quickly.

During the night, rain woke me. It was a steady rain with no thunder and lightning. I remembered not to touch the canvas of the tent to start a drip coming from overhead and went back to sleep. The next morning, I was awakened by Curt's laughter, his distinctive happy, humming sounds. Such a joy, I thought, and then I heard the slapping, splashing sounds. Our air mattress was surrounded by water flowing through the tent. Curt always loved playing in water and was happily swishing his hands around in the water and giggling.

Why do I remember this so many years later? When I stop to compare this trip with others, I remember the year that Curt choked on lobster during dinner at the campsite, and we headed to the ER. Now, I realize that was an early sign of problems with his esophagus that re-occurred later in his life, but those are memories associated with his medical issues and are part of my intellectualizing and trying to figure out something. This trip with one car, limited supplies, and a whole lot of water and laughter is a deeper, sweeter memory, and one of seeing the world through Curt's eyes. The sound of his laughter is still one of the most satisfying sounds I've ever heard. Take time; make time for fun.

Ask for Help

"Everyone is Needing me!"

Most of the time, I eventually figure things out—practical things, like how to get a load of laundry done every day. I did learn that Tide takes out dried milk and saliva in clothes, but I still buy patterned shirts for Curt that don't show the drool. However, everyone has constraints of time, money, patience, and imagination. In general, there is more information available now through support groups, parents' organizations, the internet, and books. Let other people help. When someone says, "What can I do?" give a specific, reasonable answer like, "I can't find filters for the humidifier! Can you find them and get them for me?" Or "I would love it if you would just visit tomorrow with me while I do the laundry. You can hold the kid."

Let others help, not only because it will help you, but also because it will help them feel needed, appreciated, and part of your world—a world they may not understand. My mom helped with Curt and then his sister. She would also bring over a roast that I wouldn't have purchased, saying, "I bought this and don't have room in the freezer for it" or a package of pantyhose that "was on sale." But she rarely gave us anything unless we asked for it. So ask. Some people can give you time; others can give you things. Then write a short thank you note and have your child "decorate" it in his own way (or text or Facetime to say thank you.)

Don't do everything yourself, even if you can. "Just because you can, it doesn't mean that you have to," my sister always reminds me. Ask for help from family, friends, neighbors, support groups, churches, national organizations, and the U.S. government. (See Chapter 4. OTHERS.) The more specific you are in your request, the easier it will be for someone to say yes or no. Most people don't have a clue how to help you. They are afraid, misinformed, embarrassed, or don't want to insult or embarrass you. Observe the strengths of others and ask them to give from their bounty, whether it's baking ability, the patience to read to your child, money that will pay for a fence or a wheelchair, or meals for the family when someone is ill. Your aunt may not feel strong enough to take care of your child but might be delighted to visit and help with the laundry. Most people—that includes family members—want to help. Don't be embarrassed or a Martyr Mother; you don't have to do it all.

> NOTE: This is especially important for the many single parents reading this or if you have a partner who is not helpful. Please, actively work to develop a support network for yourself. Even if you do have a supportive spouse and family, expand your support, create a village of support!

Conclusion

Part of the problem with the word 'disabilities' is that it immediately suggests an inability to see or hear or walk or do other things that many of us take for granted. But what of people who can't feel? Or talk about their feelings? Or manage their feelings in constructive ways? What of people who aren't able to form close and strong relationships? And people who cannot find fulfillment in their lives, or those who have lost hope. Who live in disappointment and bitterness and find no joy, no love? These, it seems to me, are the real disabilities.

~Fred Rogers, *The World According to Mister Rogers: Important Things to Remember*

This story hasn't ended yet. As of November 2016, Curt has his official diagnosis: 35.8 MB interstitial deletion of the long arm of #13 chromosome: arr[hg19]13q 13.3q21.33 (35, 977, 208-71, 784, 165)X1. It certainly doesn't fit in any box and it doesn't mean we know anything more about others with the diagnosis—if there are any out there—but he is medically labeled. I intend to spend some time online trying to get information about his life into databases where it might make a difference to a parent whose infant has just been diagnosed with this rare, chromosome disorder. Curt is 50 and living in the group home that has been his home since he turned 22. He is still walking at times but spending more time in a wheelchair.

He loves music, eating, being with people he enjoys, and riding around in any car, bus, plane, truck, tractor, or boat. Hundreds of people know "that Curt sound" of hollering, humming, and the flapping of his hands. He has worn a hockey helmet for years but prefers to spin its bolts while the helmet is in his lap rather than on his head. They love his quick smile, dark eyes with thick lashes, balding head, and "grandfather" eyebrows. He has had a good life and is still very much aware and engaged. He is still an extraordinary teacher for the many individuals who come in contact with him daily and very much a part of our family, but he has his own life and world.

Here's a journal entry from a few years ago:

[9/25/15]

Curtis is now 45. I've been writing about him, discussing him with therapists, and painting bizarre pictures of him for all this time and have come to a great sigh of relief. I haven't written about him all summer and have barely seen him. It's actually not much different from anyone else's life experience. Life just is, and most of the time his life is just like anyone else's.

The more I review my life when sharing a bottle of wine with my brother or sister, we agree that our parents were not trained or particularly interested in parenting, but we survived. The laissez-faire parenting we got developed our independence, taught us to see a larger picture, and encouraged our own interests. Apparently, my style as a "Good Enough Mother" worked for Curt as well. The period of time needed to see that a child is safe, fed, nurtured and cared for

*depends upon the child. In Curt's case, he will always
need someone else to do essential things like food,
clothes and shelter, but that does not mean he is less
emotionally independent or less of a complete individual. "He's himself because everyone else is taken" or
he's "Curt being Curt." (My apologies to Oscar Wilde.)
As for parenting him, it really did mean just showing
up. The list of chores seemed long, but it was just a
list. A parent can delegate, trust others to share the
responsibilities, but it still does require showing up
and with a loving, light heart. It also helps if one sees
coincidences and allows life to flow as it will. Whether
you call it God or something else, there is an overrid-
ing, gentle, loving presence that shows up whenever
you let it. Someone may open a heavy door for us,
smile knowingly, or just say "hi" when I'm stag-
gering in the parking lot with Curt. Often a person
I've never seen before will stop and say, "Isn't that
Curtis? Hi there! I worked with him at X years ago!"
Immediately, there is a shared connection, a joy, in the
middle of the grocery store parking lot.*

I know that Curt's body has been under tremendous strain
his whole life. All these years taking medications that deplete
the kidneys and liver must burn his esophagus and digestive
tract. The hundreds of times his head has smashed into a sink
or tabletop were not concussions but have certainly caused
some damage, not only to his scalp but also probably to his
brain. Physical stress on a body that was not constructed
optimally to begin with seems totally unfair and has taken a
toll. But he's still laughing, still loving his snacks even though
they are pureed, and still being Curt. When I call his home, I

ask, "Is he being Curt?" when there is any concern about his health or emotional well-being.

We are working out new ways to be together; my expectations have changed as my energy and abilities have decreased with age. I can no longer lift him if he falls. If he's not walking well, I don't feel strong enough to support him, because he outweighs me and is very unsteady and stiff. We use his wheelchair more often and sometimes need help with transferring him. Sometimes, I joke with him and say, "You know, Curt, you may soon be pushing me in a wheelchair!" but I hope that day doesn't come soon.

[11/17/16]
Love Expands: after a visit with Curt
Yesterday I spent from 12:45 until 5 PM with Curt—4
¼ hours, mostly driving around. He seemed glad to
see me but did not jump up, start flapping his hands,
and shout, "Ma-mah!" the way he usually does.
Yesterday, he only acknowledged me with a nod.
He didn't want to go outside into the bright sunlight
that hurts his eyes, but he settled into the car and our
routine of running errands. About two hours after we'd
been together, I heard a quiet, "Ma-mah," from the
back seat. It filled me with warm, soft, melting love.

Living with Joy

What is my main theme regarding parenting an individual with special needs? Isn't it to live with joy and be present to what is? There's a lot of documentation, planning, cleaning, reminding, reviewing, endless doctors' appointments, but isn't the Big Picture just living with joy, with love? I honestly can't remember when it was, but I do remember opening the door to the crowded waiting room in our pediatrician's office one day. I had carried Curt in, but he could walk independently then. You know how everyone looks up when the door opens, then immediately looks down when they see a person who looks really sick or, in this case, different? I cased the room as quickly as everyone else evaluated us, and every seat was taken. Curt must have done the same. He headed straight for a very large woman seated opposite the door. He went right up to her, and she reached out her arms and said, "Sit right here on my lap, Precious. Your mama needs to check in at that window." She knew, and I knew she knew. No other explanations were needed. Such a gift of love in a crowded waiting room. It was nothing extraordinary, just ordinary life.

It is my son's purpose to keep me on this path of pursuing joy. I have had energy and insight that comforts me since reviewing my writings and drawings in order to compile information for this book. Snowbound winter days have provided an opportunity to settle in with my past impressions, filter through the self-absorption and complaining, and pull out meaning and joy from my life with this extraordinary person who is my son. But I am still surprised and delighted that his stories are just part of my life. Most of my writing has been about other ordinary things and people, about life stuff. Perhaps that's another book? Extraordinary? No. Curt is just part of the whole. Ordinary life is precious. It feels right, and my spirit is soaring from the sound of life and being with all my loved ones. I'm hoping that these words will have a positive effect on those who read them, especially those who really need to hear them. Please pass this along to someone who will benefit from choosing joy.

"Curt in Motorboat, 2016"

Glossary

EPIDERMOLYSIS BULOSA (EB): a group of genetic conditions that result in easy blistering of the skin and mucous membranes.

IEP: Individualized Education Program (ages 3-22), document generated by the school to provide for the least restrictive environment to meet a child's educational needs.

IDEA: Individuals with Disabilities Educational Act guaranteed that every child is entitled to equal opportunities for education from ages 3 to 22 in the least restrictive setting possible.

ISP: Individualized Service Program (ages 23 up): document generated by the Department of Developmental Services (MA) to provide care and needed services for an adult.

MORNING PAGES: a practice of stream-of-consciousness writing done first thing in the morning as described in Julia Cameron's book *The Artist's Way*.

PATTERNING: an over 40-year-old controversial treatment for neurological problems based on the concept that patterns of neurological development are sequential and that progress cannot be made until each step is complete. It involves putting the body through repetitive motions to integrate patterns of response.

PEOPLE FIRST LANGUAGE: WORCESTER, MA, CITY OFFICE OF DISABILITIES: Proper etiquette when addressing a person with a disability/People First Words with Dignity: a person ... who is physically disabled, deaf or hard of hearing, in a wheelchair/ who uses a wheelchair, who is developmentally disabled, with a cognitive/intellectual disability, with a birth anomaly, congenital disability, etc.

WORDS NOT TO USE:

- Handicap
- Deaf and dumb
- Wheelchair bound, confined to a wheelchair
- Retard, mentally defective
- Birth defect

PRN: for prescription medication, a directive to give to patient as needed.

RETT SYNDROME (RTT): a genetic brain disorder which typically becomes apparent after 6 to 18 months of age, mostly in females. Symptoms include problems with language, coordination, and repetitive movements. Often there is slower growth, problems walking, and a smaller head size.

SPED: Special Education Director in public school systems.

SPINA BIFIDA: a congenital abnormality where there is incomplete closing of the backbone and membranes around the spinal cord. Associated problems include poor ability to walk, problems with bladder or bowel control, accumulation of fluid in the brain (hydrocephalus), a tethered spinal cord, and latex allergy. Learning problems are relatively uncommon.

STATUS EPILEPTICUS: a seizure that lasts longer than 5 minutes or a series of seizures that occur close together and the person is not able to recover in between them.

STAYCATION: a period in which a family stays home and engages in leisure activities within driving distance but does not go away from home overnight. It was popularized in response to recent financial crises.

THALIDOMIDE: fifty years ago, the sedative Thalidomide was withdrawn after thousands of mothers gave birth to disabled babies. Thalidomide has strong sedative properties, and many women in the early weeks of pregnancy had taken it to ease their morning sickness, utterly unaware its effect on the unborn child. Today, there are 6,000 estimated survivors around the world.

TMJ (Temporomandibular Joint Syndrome): pain in the jaw bone from tension or misalignment.

TONIC CLONIC SEIZURE: a type of seizure when the body becomes stiff with a loss of consciousness, followed by a phase of body jerks and spasms, formerly called "grand mal" seizure.

TRANSCENDENTAL MEDITATION: a technique for inner peace and wellness founded by Maharishi Makesh Yogi, www.tm.org.

References/Inspiration

BURCAW, SHANE: *Laughing at my Nightmare* (2014)

BOWLING, DUSTI: *Insignificant Events in the Life of a Cactus (2017)*

CAMERON, JULIA: *The Artist's Way (2006)*

DRAPER, SHARON M, *Out of My Mind* (2012)

EASTERSEALS.COM: *Myths and Facts about People with Disabilities*

EDWARDS, KIM: *The Memory Keeper's Daughter (2006)*

ENGEL, RICHARD: Lessons from war on raising a special needs son: To help him, we must also help ourselves. https://www.nbcnews.com/think/opinion/lessons-war-raising-special-needs-son-help-him-we-mu st-ncna853841. Find even more at NBCNews.com Richard Engel https://www.nbcnews.com/think/opinion/lessons-war-raising-special-needs-son-help-him-we-must-ncna853841 and at NBCNews.com

FUSSELL, SANDY: *Shaolin Tiger (2011)*

GARDNER, HOWARD: *Multiple Intelligences* (2008) proposed seven abilities/intelligences:

1. musical-rhythmic

2. visual-spatial

3. verbal-linguistic

4. logical-mathematical

5. bodily-kinesthetic

6. interpersonal

7. intrapersonal

He later suggested that *existential* and *moral* intelligences may also be worthy of inclusion.

GIBRAN, KAHLIL: *The Prophet* (1961), a classic, note the chapter on "Children."

McKAY AND FANNING: *Self Esteem* (2000)

MUTCH, MARIA: *Know the Night: A Memoir of Survival in the Small Hours (2014)*

MEYER, DON *(editor): Thicker than Water: Essays by Adult Siblings of People with Disabilities. (2009)*

ROGERS, FRED: *The World According to Mr. Rogers: Important Things to Remember (2010)*

SINGER, MICHAEL: *The Untethered Soul, the Journey Beyond Yourself* (2007)

SYLER, RENE: *Good Enough Mother, The Perfectly Imperfect Book of Parenting* (2007)

Some of My Favorite Movies

"The Miracle Worker" (1962)

"Being There" (1979)

"Rain Man" (1988)

"My Left Foot" (1989)

"Awakening" (1990)

"Lorenzo's Oil" (1992)

"Benny and Joon" (1993)

"What's Eating Gilbert Grape" (1993)

"Forrest Gump" (1994)

"I Am Sam" (2001)

"Mozart and the Whale" (2005)

"Temple Grandin" (2010)

"The Theory of Everything" (2014)

"Wonder" (2017)

About the Author

Lucy Mueller is a retired art therapist and teacher living in Sunapee, NH. She enjoys being an artist, writer, parent, and grandparent.

She published *Printmaking as Therapy: Frameworks for Freedom* (2002) as Lucy Mueller White.

CPSIA information can be obtained
at www.ICGtesting.com
Printed in the USA
BVHW061534060421
604345BV00008B/844